I0567655

Food Is Love

Hugh Hollowell

Canebrake Studio

Copyright ©2025 by Hugh L. Hollowell, Jr

All rights reserved.

No portion of this book may be reproduced in any form without written permission from the publisher or author, except as permitted by U.S. copyright law.

For privacy reasons, some names, locations, and dates may have been changed.

ISBN: 979-8-9940587-0-1

Published by Canebrake Studio | http://canebrakestudio.com

Author's note: No generative AI or LLM was used in the writing of this book.

Scripture quotations taken from The Holy Bible, New International Version® NIV®

Copyright © 1973, 1978, 1984, 2011 by Biblica, Inc.

Used with permission. All rights reserved worldwide.

CONTENTS

It seems to me that our three basic needs, for food and security and love, are so mixed and mingles and entwined that we cannot straightly think of one without the others. So it happens that when I write of hunger, I am really writing about love and the hunger for it, and warmth and the love of it and the hunger for it... and then the warmth and richness and fine reality of hunger satisfied... and it is all one. – M.F.K Fisher *The Art of Eating*

Better a small serving of vegetables with love than a fattened calf with hatred. – Proverbs 15:17

This one is for Renee.
(It all is for Renee)

ABOUT THIS BOOK

This book had its origins in 2020, when I, like so many of us, was stuck at home during the beginning of the COVID-19 pandemic. We were locked down in the house we had bought the year before, in a city where we knew virtually no one.

We loved this house for many reasons, but a major selling point was the huge dining room. We loved having people over, and our last house didn't have a dining room at all. I love cooking for folks I love – a way to pay back the universe for all the meals I have eaten by all the other people who loved me.

But now I was stuck at home, cooking for just us, and our dining room was quiet.

I began to process the loss of people around my table on my blog, and began to write stories about meals I loved, and the people who cooked them for me because they loved me.

We were foster parents during that time, and for most of that year were custodians of a 7-year-old boy. His name began with the letter P, and he had come to live with us on the 25th of January. So, every month after that, the 25th was known as P-Day, and we would make him a small cake, and he got to pick what we ate for supper. The joy on his face was always palpable – P-Day was always the best day of the month for us, no matter the month.

Sharing food with people you love is an act of love itself.

In the chapter called *Alchemy*, I open it having bought a sausage and biscuit at a McDonalds in Charlotte, NC. It was in December of 2021, and I was on my way home from the funeral of my friend Jess, who had died as a result of her depression. I had been her mentor when we had lived in Raleigh but then I had moved away, and now I was carrying a great deal of loss and guilt as I sat in that McDonalds' drive-thru. I was about to get on the road and needed a shot of comfort before facing the 10-hour drive home. It was not lost on me that the most comforting thing I could think of in my hours of despair was a biscuit.

On the drive home, I wrote the *Alchemy* chapter in my head. I thought about all the ways people had loved me and had shown that love by feeding me. I thought about all the people I had loved and who were now gone, and I realized that most of the memories I had of them were in some way tied to food. I also realized it worked the other way, too. The memories of them were unlocked when I ate that food – I cannot ever eat a biscuit that I do not think of Aunt Monty and her biscuits in that North Mississippi kitchen 45 years ago. I cannot eat a whop-um biscuit and not think of my Granny Pat. Every time I eat vanilla ice cream, I think of Aunt Louise.

Over the years since that trip, I have jotted the stories and recipes down – some of them have appeared on my blog, and others have been shared with the membership team that supports my writing.

Every one of these chapters were originally written as stand alone essays, so pardon any redundancy.

In these pages, you will meet all those people, and hear those stories. On one level, this is a cookbook – there are almost 30 recipes in here of foods that matter to me, that were handed to me and that have stories attached to them. On another level, it's a memoir of sorts, a putting down of stories that shaped me and my attitudes toward food.

But finally, it's about love, and how we show up for the people we love. And for my people, that usually means showing up with a plate in your hand.

ABOUT THE RECIPES

I have a collection of over 100 cookbooks filled with recipes. And the first time I make a new-to-me dish, I follow it slavishly. And then, especially if I liked the dish, I never use it again.

In my world, recipes are launchpads—points of reference, but not holy writ. I always follow them to the letter the first time, because I want to know what it's "supposed" to taste like, what the creator of the recipe imagined and then tried to capture. But after that, it's game on.

My mother would get frustrated by the people who tried to teach her to cook a dish—they said things like "Add enough flour" or "a bit of pepper"-measurements only learned by experience. And when her experience was not up to the task, the steak and gravy or the dumplings did not measure up to the original. It couldn't.

I hesitated to add written recipes to this book, because that isn't how I cook, and it isn't how the food in this book was originally made.

But if we don't share things like traditions and recipes, they get lost. So, I have written the recipes of dishes as I made them. Some of them have changed over time, but this is the current iteration. I might make it differently next time.

Also, sometimes ingredients might be scarce. You can make chicken and dressing with breakfast sausage if you don't have any chicken. You can make beef and vegetable soup with chicken instead of beef. If you substitute blueberries for the blackberries in a cobbler, nobody will know, and everyone will want the recipe.

Fresh ingredients are also variable, and non-standardized. Garlic cloves are not uniformly shaped. Let your ancestors show you the way. Do you like garlic, and your garlic cloves are small? Use more than the recipe calls for. If your garlic cloves are large, but you don't like garlic much, use less.

In short, this is not mathematics; it's jazz. Feel free to improvise, to play around, to make them your own. I don't have ownership over any recipe in this book—they were handed down to me, and so I hand them to you. Play with them and make them your own. Pass them down to your children, make them at Thanksgiving or birthdays or just because it's Thursday. I hope you will use them to make food for the people you love, and I hope the memories from those meals remind you of the love that was the key ingredient.

INTRODUCTION

This is a book about food, but it is more than that - it is a book about love.

It's a record of the stories I know about the food that I love, and the people who loved me enough to share it with me. It is not coincidental that every single food I love has a story to go with it. The stories make the food taste better, I am convinced, and while I recognize there are people who are so disconnected from their roots that they regularly eat food that comes with no stories, that doesn't mean I don't pray for those people, and recognize that their lives are the poorer for it, and am reminded once again that not everyone was born with the advantages I have had.

The food in this book is food made for working people, by working people. The food found in these pages is delicious, but not ever fancy. It was made for people - generally, but not exclusively, men - who had worked hard all day, and who would get up early and work hard again all day tomorrow. And it was made by people - generally, but not exclusively, women - who would work hard all day to scrimp pennies and wrangle children and turn scraps and leftovers and rejects into sustenance.

For the most part, the food in this book was made by and for people who had known hard times, and who were determined to survive. These were lives where things like "happiness" and "joy" got pushed aside to make room for things like "survival" and "perseverance." After a day of hard work for little pay, eating an inexpensive supper made up of biscuits and milk gravy with sausage might well be the bright spot of that day. If there was a small slice of orange cake left over from the potluck supper at the church to finish it all off, all the better. It wasn't just that the food was cheap and good - it was enough to make you think you could make it another day.

I like to point out the working-class roots of this food because that often gets lost. I was in a city on the East Coast some years ago and saw "cheese grit cutlets" being sold at a southern fusion joint - a meal my people would have recognized instantly as fried grits, a routine breakfast in their homes on mornings when there were leftover grits from the day before. They would not have recognized the "infused honey butter" it was served with, nor known what to do with the $24.95 price tag.

I am not alone in this - I feel a kinship to the Mexican brick layer who sees taco bars spring up in neighborhoods lived in by people who vote for policies that ensure people like him can never afford to live there or afford to eat there.

Well, well, well. It got political all of a sudden. When can we go back to talking about food, Hugh?

Don't be fooled. Food is always political. Always.

Being able to feed yourself and your family means being able to determine your future. It gives you agency and power. As fellow

Mississippian Fannie Lou Hamer once said, "When you've got 400 quarts of greens and gumbo soup canned for the winter, nobody can push you around or tell you what to say or do." The oligarchs learned long ago that hungry people don't fight back.

The health, energy, rejuvenation, and even joy that comes from simple food, prepared well, can give downtrodden people enough margin in their lives to keep going and sometimes inch forward, even when everything around them seems to conspire against them.

It has been pointed out to me by people who are concerned about such things that the foods in this collection tend to be heavy in fat, and tend to be fried. There are reasons for this.

The most obvious is that this is a collection of the foods that stir memories of comfort and community for me, and those foods happen to be fried and caloric. So there is some bias there - much like it wouldn't make sense to question why a collection of recipes of foods from children's birthday parties had so much sugar in it. But that's not the whole story – you must dig deeper.

And when you do, you realize that in the first place, fat was by far the most calorically dense of the three major macro-nutrients (fat, protein, and carbohydrates), and has historically been cheap, so if you are poor and need energy, fat was the cheapest and easiest way to get it.

But you also learn that poor folks - especially poor folks in the South - have always learned how to make do with the foods nobody else wanted. Enslaved folks learned how to cook and eat chitterlings (don't fight me - it's spelled that way, even though it's pronounced "chitlins" - sort of like how the word colonel isn't spelled the way it sounds, either) because the chitterlings was what was left over from the meal in the big house, where they were eating pork tenderloin, and about the only way you can make a chitterling taste like anything you want to eat is to fry it. (I know some folk that eat them boiled, but I know some folk that also put ketchup on their black-eyed peas. I have long since given up trying to change people - all you can do is try to love them.)

You get that? They took scraps off the oligarch's table and made them into cuisine. They turned trash into sustenance. They took the waste of Empire and turned it into the means of their flourishing and the perpetuation of their line.

See? Political again. Shrug.

And because this food was then combined with love and care for people the cooks loved, it made not just calories but memories, and if this book has any point to make at all, it is that memories are tied to food.

Your favorite meal is not the healthiest meal you ever ate. It is not even the best meal you ever ate. It is the one with the best memories attached to it. My people built memories around foods that nobody else wanted, meals made from scraps and then consecrated with love and attention and that thus entered into sacramental territory in our own personal family liturgies.

But by far a much larger factor is that because we tend to tie food to memories - and mostly good memories at that - the food we tend to have the most positive associations with is the food of celebrations.

The people who taught us to love fried chicken did not eat fried chicken every day - Chickens were a valuable part of the farm ecosystem, and one did not just kill them and then put the hours of work into plucking, butchering, marinating and then frying them because it was Thursday. No, you did that to celebrate something: A birthday, a holy day, or maybe the preacher coming over for supper after the revival preaching. Before the Colonel opened his chicken joint, a working family might only eat fried chicken three or four times a year.

In much the same way that we now generally recognize that chocolate cake is not healthy, but also recognize that most people don't regularly eat it except for three or four times a year at celebrations, many of the foods we now villainize as unhealthy were the foods of celebration. It wasn't how they ate every day.

Some of the food in this book - like eggs and biscuits and gravy - might be eaten every week. Some of it, like cobblers and fudge pies or chicken and dressing - might only get made for holidays and celebrations. But it is the people that make the celebration, not the food. I have been to parties catered with fancy food that were sterile and lifeless, and parties where we ate homemade tamales and sheet cake that came from the bakery in Walmart that I hope I remember until I die.

This is also a book about joy. A book about celebration. A book about survival, perseverance, and endurance in the struggle. A book about hope, and a belief that what we do today matters, even as we work to make sure the future is different.

In the end, this is a book about love.

1

THE OLD MAGIC

In that kitchen I learned about alchemy - the practice, if not the word.

If I close my eyes, I can see the light filtered through the handmade green gingham curtains that move with the breeze. I can hear the news being read over the small radio to the left of the sink, next to the snuffbox.

It was on those worn linoleum tiles, peeping over the edge of the counter, on my knees on the green vinyl chair, that I watched it happen—the battered aluminum bowl, the scoops of flour, the sweet milk, the knob of Crisco the size of an unshelled walnut.

Done without measurement, the muscle memory made deep by years of daily practice making biscuits, feeding your family for pennies.

In the old days, people believed that if you knew the right words, you could turn base metal into gold, but in that kitchen, I learned the deeper truth, the even older magic: That with time and intention, you could turn flour into food, scraps into sufficiency, and ingredients into love.

2

ALCHEMY

When I pulled out of the cheap motel on the outskirts of Charlotte, NC, I couldn't wait to hit the road, with 10 hours of between me and home. But first, I had to refuel. I grabbed some gas at the gas station and spied a McDonald's across the way. Say what you will about them, but they are reliable, if nothing else. I grabbed a sausage biscuit and coffee and hit the road.

I must confess – it wasn't all that good, but then, I hadn't expected that it would be. Reliable, though. Like, you know how bad it's going to be in advance, and can brace yourself for it.

I know a thing or two about biscuits, having eaten them all my life. Like the French have baguettes, biscuits are the bread of my people and my culture. And as often happens when I eat food that is filled with memories, I reflect on previous meals I have had with that same food. And perhaps no food has more memories attached to it for me, in as many places as do biscuits.

I do not recall my momma ever making biscuits, though. In her defense, she wasn't a natural cook. She married way too young, after a childhood of moving often as part of a military family. She had no traditions when she married dad. Dad's mom died shortly after that. And we had to make it on our own, with nothing but church cookbooks, Southern Living, some elderly neighbors that loved us, and the back of boxes to guide us.

Mom never really enjoyed cooking. It was a thing she did, but you got no feeling she derived any pleasure from the act, nor appreciated the attention that comes from doing it well. It was a chore to be done, like washing the dishes or sweeping the floor, and gave her about as much pleasure as either of those tasks.

But Dad – now Dad could make a hell of a biscuit. Big, fluffy cathead biscuits, big as your fist. He didn't do it often, but when he did, they were amazing. I remember weekend mornings when Dad would make breakfast – rarely, because when he worked for the gas company he worked Saturday mornings, and up until 14 or so we went to church regular as a family (one day, I'll have to tell you the story of why we stopped. Or maybe not – some things are best handled around a table, late into the night). But when he did, you knew you were about to get fed. As a child, he taught me to make biscuits and scrambled eggs, because then you could always feed yourself for cheap, he told me.

My mom's stepmother was a tiny woman who had grown up in the city, and while she loved me fiercely, she couldn't make a biscuit either. When we would go visit them in the summertime outside Dallas Texas, she would make sausage gravy and whop-um biscuits – called that because to open the can, you whopped um on the side of the counter – and they were a novelty for us. They were the cheap canned biscuits, small and round and flat topped, with a layered nature one never saw in a real biscuit. It almost felt like eating desert.

In the Marines, the mess hall would have biscuits, but they were square, for some reason known only to God and the Commandant, and I'm sorry, but you can't really enjoy a square biscuit, even if it didn't taste of too much baking powder, which these did.

Some years back, Renee got a biscuit cookbook and learned how to make amazing biscuits, a lot like the ones Dad made all those years ago. And they are huge and puffy and have little peaks and knobs, and because they are made with love and practice by someone who loves me, I love them.

But my platonic ideal of a biscuit is none of those.

Her name was Montaree, but we all called her Aunt Monty (pronounced Ain't Monny). She and her husband Doc lived in a 900 square foot house they built on three acres my grandmother had sold them when our money was tight. My Aunt Louise's husband had built and wired the house for them, and it had pine floors coated with amber shellac. And growing up, Monty and Doc played the role in my life grandparents would have traditionally, had my folks not all died off when I was little.

Monty made biscuits every morning of her life up until Doc died and she moved to be with her son in Jackson. But that wouldn't be until after I left – my whole childhood, she made biscuits. She had a five-gallon sized metal bucket, with a tight fitting lid, she kept in the cabinet under the counter that she kept her flour in—self-rising flour bought in 25-pound sacks made from cloth, that had a dish towel that came with it as a premium. I don't think she ever had a purpose-bought dish towel when I knew her.

She had a large bowl not used for anything other than biscuit making, and she would scoop out flour from the bucket, and put it in the bowl, making a depression in the middle of the pile of flour, into which she took a small lump of lard in the winter (after the hog killing) or shortening in the summer (after the lard ran out) and massaged it all in, so it looked like corn meal when she was done. To this she added sweet milk a splash at a time until it was right, and then massaged it into a wad of dough.

She then floured the countertop and patted out the dough until it was thin and used a tin can with the ends cut out (that resided in the flour bucket, along with the biscuit bowl when not in use) to cut out the biscuits. She would place the biscuits on a small cookie sheet, perhaps 8×16, that was so old its origins were lost to history, and before putting them in the oven would smear a light coat of whatever grease she was using, lard or shortening, on top.

I must have watched her do it a hundred times. There would always be scraps of dough left over, which she would fashion into a small freeform biscuit that was meant for me.

These were not elegant biscuits. They were not even all that pretty. They were flat, perhaps ¾ of an inch thick, the size of a regular tin can, with none of the knobs and bumps of the biscuits Dad made, the like of which I saw in magazines. These were lightly browned on the bottom and golden on the edges of the top, and had a crumb that reminds one visually, but not texturally, of English muffins.

These were not fancy biscuits but daily biscuits, which fed a well digger for 50 years and were literally their daily bread. It was the bread with their meals – they were made fresh and eaten hot for lunch, their big meal, and leftovers were eaten cold at supper and for breakfast. I can close my eyes and smell the hot bread and the plum jelly, made from the wild plums by the fence line, and feel the melting butter run over my fingers and drop off my chin.

In later years I would, in an old book found in the school library, learn about alchemy - the pseudo-science that claims base ingredients could, through magic and intention, become valuable. It was dismissed by the author of that book as ludicrous, but I didn't have to be convinced. Flour. Milk. Shortening. Simple cheap ingredients that, once mixed together with intention and love, made something magical. I had eaten a biscuit made by the hands of someone who loved me, and thus I knew the truth.

I love to cook. I derive pleasure from it, and pleasure from being good at it, and while I can make a passable biscuit, I have never been able to make a biscuit like Monty's. Lord knows I've tried. Hell, I've never even seen another one like it.

I guess those biscuits will just have to live in my memory. But right after we bought this house, one of the first things I did was plant some wild plums out by the fence line.

3

MAKING YOUR OWN LUCK

Growing up in and shaped by the hills of North Mississippi and loved and fed by land-owning members of the working class, we ate simple food. So, the food of our celebrations was also simple, although given a bit more time and intention.

The holidays spanned a period that began at Thanksgiving and continued through New Year's Day. A liturgical procession of meals came with the holidays: Chicken and dressing. Fudge pies. Giant hams studded with cloves and pineapple slices. Homemade cranberry sauce. It was a magical time when people would pop by with repurposed tins of fudge squares - with a pecan half pressed firmly in each square - made in their kitchens because they had no money to purchase store bought gifts.

And on New Year's Day, we wrapped it up with a big pot of black-eyed peas and a side of collard greens.

All food is regional, and all food is cultural. And I know they eat corned beef and cabbage north of here to celebrate the calendar's new start. In the Low Country of South Carolina and Georgia, they eat Hopping John - a thick, rich soup of rice and black-eyed peas. But my people in the hills on the far western border of Southern Appalachia ate black-eyed peas, ham, collards, and cornbread on New Year's Day. For luck, you know. That we live in a historically and persistently economically depressed area that has been perennially unlucky is not lost on me, but what can you do? Hope springs eternal.

I must confess that I do not know that eating black-eyed peas is actually lucky. Luck was not the sort of thing my people looked for. Instead, as my daddy said, we tended to play the hands we were dealt. A melancholy resignation came with our lot in life - one born of fatigue and experience and too many broken dreams.

But I do know that people who loved me made this meal for me. They spent time and effort to make it taste special. They infused simple broth and beans with love and a sort of bedraggled hopefulness, and they taught me that engaging in pleasure when times are hard is a way of making your own luck.

So, when I eat this meal of black-eyed peas and collards, which were first prepared for me by the old people who cared for me, I am reminded of happy times and the purest love I have ever known.

If we want to keep traditions alive, we must make room for them. And any tradition that involves sitting down to a meal, made with care and love, that marks the entry point into a new time with hope and intention is a tradition worth preserving.

So, on New Year's, we still eat black-eyed peas and collards in my house.

Let's get things straight: black-eyed peas aren't peas. They're beans, as sure as anything, brought to the States from Africa as feed for enslaved Africans on ships in the horrifying Middle Passage. Once here, those seeds were planted, and the beans were used to feed enslaved people and livestock. The poor whites who constituted much of the South and who ate scraps the wealthy left behind learned to eat them too. During Reconstruction, pretty near everyone was eating them. Over time, centuries of memory and meaning infused them with magical powers.

In addition, they taste good.

Since they are beans, they must be cooked like beans. In fact, you can cook them just like the pintos I have described elsewhere in these pages and have an entirely acceptable dish. But since this is New Year's, after all, I tend to fancy it up. The collards are an accommodation I have developed over time since I'm the only person in my house who likes them, so cooking up a large pot doesn't make much sense.

Doing it this way makes enough for 12 polite folks or eight hungry ones. But it halves perfectly if you don't have a lot of people to feed.

You need to get a few things before we get started.

Traditionally, you would have the ham bone leftover from your Christmas ham, hopefully with about two pounds of meat still on it. If you didn't save leftovers and the bones from your Christmas ham, you can (and should) buy in two pounds of smoked ham hock, or if you find yourself in a part of the world where you can't easily buy ham hock, dice up a couple of pounds of bacon.

Two pounds of dried black-eyed peas. As I said earlier, the thing about black-eyed peas is that they're beans. So, you should soak them, but you don't have to. They don't need a lot of soaking, and some folks don't soak black-eyed peas at all. But I generally soak mine for a couple of hours. Just spread them out on a cookie sheet, sort them for dirt and debris, then put them in a stockpot with enough cold water to cover them by about two inches.

Salt. People get fancy with their salt these days, but I use kosher salt for cooking and iodized salt for the table. So, you do you – salt is salt, and best done to taste anyway.

A large onion, as big as your fist.

Cloves. You want whole cloves here, and hopefully you already have some from when you made the Christmas ham. If not, see if you can borrow some from a neighbor, but if not, buy the smallest container you can. You only need a couple.

A bay leaf. I feel like this can be left out, but I love this dish so much I'm afraid to try subtracting things.

Ground black pepper. Just like you have in the pepper shaker.

Allspice. I picked this up a few years ago and loved the depth it adds to the dish. I doubt my ancestors would have known what this was, let alone add it to a pot of beans, but I recommend it. Traditions change, but slowly, mostly around the edges and over time.

Vegetable oil. Just plain old corn oil works fine, as does Canola. Use what you have.

Four nice-sized garlic cloves. Honestly, the four is a guesstimate. I would use at least four, but sometimes the spirit catches me, and I might go as high as six or seven. I do love some garlic.

Crushed red pepper.

Two bunches of collard greens. My people would just said "a mess of collards," but I'm assuming you are going to the store, and they will look at you funny if you asked for that. The stores tend to sell them in 1-pound bunches, and you need about two pounds of greens.

When I started talking about collard greens, some of y'all tuned your nose up, thinking you are too good to eat collard greens. In my experience, people who think this way about collards often have no problem eating kale on anything that isn't nailed down.

Get over yourself. Kale and Collards are practically siblings, both just being unheaded cabbage. If you can't get collards, you can use kale in this recipe, but don't tell anybody I said so. But collards are traditional, and if you are too snooty to eat them and end up unlucky this year because you did it wrong, don't come crying to me.

You did clean and soak your peas, right? If not, go back and do that. Then drain your peas and put them back in the stockpot. Dice up your meat (including the skin and fat) into pieces about an inch or two in size and add them and the bone to the pot. If you are using the bone (and you should) don't worry about cleaning it off – the meat will fall off it as it cooks. Some folks are panicking over the mention of ham skin here but trust me on this – it will melt and meld into something approaching heaven before we are done. Next, put in enough cold water to cover the beans about two inches and set the heat as high as it will go.

While waiting for it to boil, peel your onion and stick 2 cloves in it. Cloves are pointy, and you can just push them into the onion like thumbtacks. You will remove the onion later, which makes it easier, but I have also just tossed the cloves in the pot, sliced the onion fine, and left it in, which works too. It's mostly a matter of opinion, and this way involves less chopping and tears. Add the onion, ½ a teaspoon of allspice, ½ a teaspoon of the black pepper, the bay leaf, and a teaspoon of salt to the water and bring it to a boil. We will probably add more salt later, but depending on what meat you used, it may already be salty, and too much salt will ruin a dish. As my momma says, adding more is easier than taking it out.

After it comes to a boil, turn your heat down and let it simmer. Stir them every 10 or 15 minutes, just as you pass through the kitchen, and check your water levels at the same time. The water will cook away, so keep adding water to keep at least an inch of water over the peas.

Cooking times will vary depending on how fresh the peas are and how your stove cooks, but after about an hour and a half, start checking to see if the peas are tender. They generally take me about two hours to be right. They are done when a pea will mash evenly between your fingers. If nobody's looking, you can taste it – they shouldn't be crunchy but firm. Nobody wants mushy peas. The broth will be rich and dark and should be tasted at this point for salt. I often put about another two teaspoons in here, but go by taste, adding a bit, stirring a bit, and tasting as you go.

Remove the bone and the onion if you left it whole, and discard them, but only after picking the bone clean.

About an hour and a half into the beans cooking, it's time to make the collards.

First, they need to be rinsed. Dirt likes to get in the crevices of the leaves, so rinse them well under running water. You can shake the water off them, but don't dry them in a salad spinner or anything – they need some moisture to cook. Next, cut out the big pieces of the stem and discard them. Take the leaves, roll them like cigars, and then slice them into one-inch-wide strips. Peel and mince your garlic now as well.

In a big (at least 10 inch, but 12 is better) skillet, add your vegetable oil and coat the bottom of the skillet with it, turning the skillet one way and another. Then put it over high heat and watch the oil – when it turns wavy it's time to cook.

Add your garlic and a ½ teaspoon of crushed red pepper to the oil and sauté it around, letting it sizzle – but don't let it brown. After 30 seconds or so, when it smells amazing, add in the collard greens and stir them around in the oil, so they get coated. I sprinkle about a ¼ teaspoon of salt on them now, and then add a cup of water, stirring the greens around in it. This will begin to wilt the greens, which is what we are going for. Turn the heat down to medium and then put a lid on the skillet, leaving it slightly cracked so steam can escape. Let it cook for about 20 minutes, softening the greens, but not disintegrating them.

On New Year's Day, I generally plate these up and take them to the table rather than serving family style, but I guess you could. I put the black-eyed peas and some meat in a bowl with lots of broth and then scatter the greens over the top, but this is controversial amongst my people. Some folks prefer them served on a plate, drained, with the collards to the side.

Either way, I would make some cornbread to go with it. If company was coming over, I might serve it with corn sticks instead of cornbread because we are fancy like that.

When eaten as part of a celebration, I will serve vanilla ice cream along with the blackberry cobbler I have described elsewhere in these pages for dessert.

What could feel luckier than that?

Black-eyed peas and ham

Ingredients

- 2 pounds black-eyed peas (soaked about 2 hours for best results)

- 2 pounds leftover ham, or smoked ham hock, or a meaty ham bone or bacon

- 2 teaspoons kosher salt

- 1 large onion, peeled and stuck with several (2-3) cloves

- 1 bay leaf

- ½ teaspoon black pepper

- ½ teaspoon allspice

Drain the peas and put them in a pot. Add the meat or ham bone or bacon. Cover this with about 2 inches of water and turn the heat to high. Add the salt, the onion stuck with cloves, bay leaf, black pepper, and allspice.

Bring it to a boil, then reduce the heat to a simmer. Simmer it for 1 1/2 to 2 hours, until the peas are tender. As it cooks, add water as necessary, always keeping the peas covered with about an inch or so of liquid, stirring occasionally.

When the peas are tender, turn off the heat. Check for salt and add more if it needs it. This will be pretty brothy. Remove the meat from the pot with a slotted spoon and chop it into bite sized pieces and set it aside for the collards.

Quick collards

Ingredients

- 2 pounds collard greens, sliced into ribbons

- 2 tablespoons vegetable oil

- 4 garlic cloves, minced

- ½ teaspoon crushed red pepper

In a large skillet over high heat, add the oil and heat until the surface of the oil shimmers. Add the minced garlic and the red pepper to the oil and sauté, not letting it brown.

At this point, add the collard greens and stir in the oil/garlic/pepper mixture. Sprinkle with a generous pinch of salt, and then add a cup of water while stirring the collards. Then put the chopped meat in the skillet, reduce the heat to medium, partially cover, and cook until greens are soft, about 20 minutes.

4

THE NAME IS THE RECIPE

My Aunt Louise was a fierce, tiny no-nonsense sort of woman, who lived alone on 40 acres, some 50 miles from the nearest city of any consequence. She could not drive, carried a pistol in her purse, and was determined to make her own life. She was my father's mother's sister, and she loved me.

She lived in the house her husband had left her when he died the year I was born, and there she and her two dogs, Festus and Princess, tried to carve out a life. Money was tight, and there was no one to impress, so she designed her life to suit her. And often, if I spent the night at her house, she would fix soup.

Sometimes it was just something from a can - sometimes tomato and sometimes bean and bacon, but often it was chicken noodle. Now, if you have had chicken noodle condensed soup, you know it is a sad affair, just broth with a hint of chicken and the tiniest noodles one can imagine. It nearly suffers the same affliction that Grape Nuts does, which contains neither Grapes nor Nuts.

But the ritual of it all captured me: The opening of the can, the stirring of the soup in the pot, served in a bowl that sat on a plate, where you put your crackers - and there were always crackers. It taught me that you can find meaning and comfort in the meanest of meals if you look for it and if it is prepared with intention and love.

In fact, the thing I remember most about eating chicken noodle soup at Aunt Louise's was her griping about how scant both chicken and noodles were. But living alone, so far from town, unable to drive, she had to make do.

Luckily, most of us do not have that restriction. As an adult, I learned to make chicken noodle soup that would fill you up, would take minutes to make, and tasted amazing. Soup is also one of the cheapest things you can make, comprising the leftovers of other things. And it reduces waste as well, using up scraps you would be otherwise tempted to throw away.

I debated whether even to include such a thing as chicken noodle soup in this collection, as most of the ingredients are in the name of the thing (sort of like the way the recipe for Peanut Butter and Jelly Sandwich is in the name). Soup is less of a recipe and more of a way of thinking about things. But I decided to include it as an example, and at worst, you can have great soup to eat, and at best, it will give you a jumping-off place.

The main ingredients in chicken noodle soup are, well, chicken and noodles. See? You can't really mess this up. I often find myself making chicken noodle soup with the leftover chicken after we have had chicken for supper - like the chicken and dressing I talk about elsewhere in these pages. But it is also perfectly acceptable to just go to the grocery store and buy yourself a rotisserie chicken from the deli counter. There is nothing wrong with this, and much that's right with it.

In a perfect world, you would have a mixture of white and dark meat, chopped up small pieces of skin as well, and chopped into pieces all about the size of the first joint of your thumb. In other words, bite-sized pieces, but if your leftover chicken doesn't lend itself to this, do the best you can. Nobody wins prizes based on how their soup looks - it's the taste we're after here. If you have about two cups of chicken when all is said and done, you're fine.

And you will need broth. If you have the time, you can take about six chicken thighs or legs, put them in water, along with some chopped up carrots and celery, and bring it all to a boil. Put a lid on it, turn the heat off and let it cool down for an hour and then you have both broth and chicken, but such an idea defeats the purpose of this being chicken soup in a hurry.

Or perhaps you are industrious and have saved your bones and vegetable scraps, made chicken broth, and then frozen it in quart containers in your deep freeze. But you probably didn't. Many of us will be using chicken broth from a can, or chicken base paste (which sounds horrible, but tastes amazing) such as Better Than Bouillon, or even, in an emergency, a bouillon cube. We need about 7 cups of broth, whatever the source.

And for the noodles, just plain old medium-width egg noodles are fine. They are sort of a secret weapon for me that are dirt cheap and always in my pantry. You are going to need about half a pound of them, or 8 ounces, if you are the type of person who needs a scale to cook.

You need some aromatics too - an onion or, if you are feeling fancy, a shallot, some carrots, a stalk of celery, and some spices you most likely already have in your cabinet, like pepper and thyme and parsley.

And that's the whole list.

The last time I made this, here's how it went:

I had been at a meeting that ran late, so I had swung by the grocery store on the way home, fighting the five o'clock crowds for a rotisserie chicken. You want the chicken cool for ease of shredding, so buying the chicken early in the day works too - just stick it in the fridge until you are ready.

I got out my big pot, put seven cups of water in it, and set it over high heat. While waiting for it to get hot, I chopped a shallot, getting about a 1/4 cup from it. I then plucked a celery stalk from the sad, wilted celery still in my crisper drawer, cleaned it, sliced it end to end, and diced it into small pieces. Both of these then went into the pot of water.

I got two carrots, chopped the ends off, peeled them, and cut them into 1/4 inch thick coins. I like my carrots to be prominent, but if you didn't. you could quarter them lengthwise before slicing - it's just a matter of aesthetics and won't affect the taste. Do know though that bigger pieces are easier to pick out if you have a picky eater in your house. Add them to the pot.

I don't always have chicken stock on hand and rarely buy it in cans, as it always seems expensive for what it is. Instead, I buy the Better Than Bullion chicken base, which is just broth concentrate, and takes 1 teaspoon of concentrate to a cup of water to make an excellent broth. I add 2 and a half Tablespoons of chicken base to the water, which is now beginning to simmer. I stir the base in, but don't fret about this too much - it just needs time to dissolve, and you will stir this a lot more before you're done.

It's time to deal with your chicken - I just pulled the chicken out of the fridge, picked the meat off the chicken and roughly chopped it, getting two cups worth of both breast and leg and some of that good rotisserie chicken skin. Throw it all into the pot.

And finally, I add a couple of teaspoons of dried parsley and about half a teaspoon each of ground thyme and black pepper. If your water is boiling now, cut it back to a mild simmer, and add about 6 ounces of noodles.

If you are feeding hungry people, you can really stretch this meal by adding more noodles here, and if you want more of a soupy soup, you can add less. Most people seem to fall in the 6-8 ounces range here, and I am firmly on the 8-ounce team, but you do you. If you are making this for the first time, start with 6 ounces and see what you think.

Stir it once more, put a lid on it, and let it simmer for 15 minutes or so, stirring it every once in a while. This makes eight polite servings (or four hungry ones) and pairs wonderfully with biscuits, corn sticks, or, of course, saltine crackers.

Elsewhere in these pages, I have written at great length about the virtues of cornbread, which some people do, admittedly, like to eat with their soup. But to me, soup calls for corn sticks.

What's that? You have never heard of corn sticks?

Mercy.

Corn sticks are a cross between cornbread and a muffin - they are lighter and sweeter than regular cornbread, but they come in individual servings like muffins. But they look like little corn ears.

Well, they do if you squint sort of hard.

When my grandmother died, I inherited her corn stick pans, which is a sort of cast iron muffin tin, but that has seven molds shaped like ears of corn. Because it's cast iron, each ear has a crispy exterior, giving you a taste you don't get in either muffins or regular cornbread.

You may not have a grandmother who will let you borrow her cast iron corn stick pan. They still sell them new - down here, you can even find them over by the cast iron skillets in Walmart. But if you are against spending $20 on a piece of kitchen equipment that will last the rest of your life, you can also make corn sticks in muffin tins. But then you don't have corn sticks anymore, of course. They are more like corn cupcakes.

If you are of a mind, you can just make a batch of cornbread batter, pour it into a corn stick pan, cook it, and have corn sticks. Sorta. But we like our corn sticks to be a bit lighter - what works great in a regular cornbread is a bit too dense in a corn stick. And the woman I am married to prefers her corn sticks (and corn muffins) to be a bit sweet, and I prefer to stay married, so when I make these, I add flour and sugar. You could, I guess, make this in a cast iron skillet and have something that looks like cornbread, but you wouldn't fool anyone and would just embarrass yourself.

Repeat after me: Sugar and flour go in corn sticks and muffins, not cornbread.

Oil your corn stick pan or muffin pan well. If you absolutely must use that spray, you can, but I generally just put a dab of oil in one of the cups and wipe it around with my finger. Put your oven at 400 degrees, and, if you are making cornsticks, put your pans in the oven to heat up. Don't do this with regular muffin pans, though, or they will warp. Ask me how I know this.

We make this with sweet milk (as opposed to buttermilk), and I'm not sure why, but that's how I was taught to do it. But it works, and I have been unwilling to mess with it. So if you try experimenting, let me know how it turns out.

In a large bowl, mix together a cup of cornmeal and a cup of flour. Fancy stone ground cornmeal doesn't buy you anything here - a finer grind will work better, as will all-purpose flour. Add a quarter cup of sugar and 1/2 teaspoon of salt, more or less, and whisk it all together. In the middle of this powdery mix, I make a well of sorts - kinda like you would when making biscuits - and then crack an egg in it, and add a cup of milk and a 1/4 cup of oil before stirring it all well with your fork or whisk.

Now, you can use any kind of oil here, but don't go crazy with olive oil or walnut oil or something: good old vegetable oil is OK, as is melted butter. But mostly, I use Canola oil for this, as it doesn't bring a flavor with it.

Don't over-mix this: It's not cake, no matter how much sugar you just put in it. Twenty or thirty strokes is plenty - you just want it mixed well. If you are making corn sticks, take the hot pans out of the oven.

Then with a large serving spoon, spoon the batter into your corn-stick pan or muffin tins, and put them in your oven for around 20 minutes. They will pop out easier if you let them cool a bit.

As an aside, if you ever find yourself in a tight place and don't know what to bring to a potluck, these are cheap to make, and everybody likes them.

Serving instructions

I like serving soup by putting the big pot on the counter, and putting a stack of bowls beside it, so people can ladle it up themselves, with the corn sticks in a towel lined basket on the table.

That said, some folks like to crumble the corn sticks in the bottom of the bowl before ladling the soup on top of it. But really, there isn't a wrong way to do this. In fact, there isn't really a wrong way to do any of this. Food is either good or not, as defined by you. It is the way you like it, or it isn't. The important thing is that it suits your needs and moves you closer to the sort of life you want to have.

And if it does that, you are rich indeed.

Chicken noodle soup

Ingredients

- 7 cups of water

- 2½ Tbsp chicken base, such as Better Than Bouillion

- 1 Tbsp finely minced shallot

- 2 large carrots, peeled and thinly sliced into coins

- 1 celery stalk, cleaned and sliced

- 2 tsp dried parsley leaves

- 1/2 tsp ground thyme

- 1/2 tsp ground pepper

- 6 oz dried medium egg noodles

- 2 cups cooked, shredded chicken in bite-sized pieces

In a large stock pot, heat the water over medium heat. Whisk in your chicken base until it's dissolved.

Add shallot, carrots, celery, and spices, and then stir. Cover with a lid and bring soup to a boil, stirring occasionally.

After it gets to a boil, reduce heat to medium-low, add noodles and chicken, and cover and simmer until about 15 minutes, stirring occasionally. Add additional broth or water to get to the consistency you want.

Corn sticks

Ingredients

- 1/4 cup sugar

- 1/2 teaspoon salt

- 1 tablespoon baking powder

- 1 cup flour

- 1 cup cornmeal

- 1/4 cup oil

- 1 large egg

- 1 cup milk

Preheat the oven to 400 degrees.

In a large bowl combine all the dry ingredients and make a well in the center. In the well, add the remaining ingredients, mixing well until all the ingredients are moistened. Do not over mix - about 20 to 30 strokes are all you need. Spoon the batter into a well-oiled muffin tin or preheated corn stick pan and bake at 400° for about 20 minutes. Allow them to cool slightly before removing from the pan.

5

NOT DIET FOOD

There is a flowering bush down here that is quite common in older, more established neighborhoods. It roots easily when cuttings are placed in water, which makes it easy to share with your friends. That, plus it being practically indestructible, means it gets shared a lot. The people sharing it often don't know that scientists call it *Hibiscus syriacus*, and everyone else pretty much calls it Rose of Sharon.

Instead, people make up their own name for the pretty bush their friend Mabel gave them all those years ago at the church plant swap. They call it something like "Fourth of July bush" because, you guessed it, it blooms around the fourth of July. Then their kids grow up and move away and think everybody calls it a Fourth of July bush, and nobody knows what they are talking about.

That process is how I figure that I never knew I was eating Salisbury steak at least once a month my whole childhood until I saw it on the menu board at the mess hall when I was in the Marines. We always just called it hamburger steak and gravy. Not to be confused with steak and gravy, which is a different beast altogether, and whose recipe is also relayed elsewhere in these pages.

If you go down a research rabbit hole, you will learn that Salisbury steak was "invented" by a man named Banting, who was obese and developed an early form of the ketogenic diet. But we didn't know anything about that in Marshall County- we just knew it was cheap to make, quick to prepare, and tasted delicious. As I have said elsewhere, my mom was not a natural cook. It was a chore for her, and this was something she made regularly and made well. So, every time I eat this, it feels like home.

We served it mostly with rice, which we ate much more often than mashed potatoes. There are a couple of reasons for that - rice kept for ages, whereas the hot and humid climate of North Mississippi precluded keeping potatoes for any length of time. Most of the mashed potatoes I ate as a kid were made from the dehydrated potato flakes in the commodities box we picked up monthly in the county seat.

Another nice thing about this meal is its adaptability to circumstances, budget, and taste. It was served most often in our house with plain brown gravy, occasionally with onions, and, more rarely, sliced mushrooms. In my opinion, it should always be served with mushrooms, but my wife, who is the primary person for whom I cook these days, and to whom I wish to remain married, disagrees with me. What are you gonna do?

If you frequent the frozen food section of the grocery store, you may come across a frozen dinner that purports to be Salisbury steak and mashed potatoes. Overcome with a wave of nostalgia, you might be tempted to purchase it and eat it on a night when you find yourself in low circumstances and need an injection of nostalgia to lift your mood.

Resist this urge with all of your powers. You will not feel better after eating the contents of that pasteboard box. All you will feel is sad and a bit angry at yourself for believing it would taste good in the first place. Especially when the real thing is so easy to make.

You start with ground beef - a pound will make four healthy servings. This is not the place to be fancy. The 73% plain ground beef is fine here. Chuck works well too. I would not use the extra lean 93% ground beef, even if I were on a diet. If you are on a diet, perhaps you picked up this book by mistake. You should demand a refund.

Crumble the ground beef into a medium-sized bowl, and then crack an egg on top of it. Add a good squirt of ketchup, about two teaspoons worth, if you are the type of person who measures things, and then about half that much Dijon mustard. If you are not the Dijon mustard type, you can use hot dog mustard here, but the Dijon mustard tastes better. Don't be scared of something new - they have it at the grocery store these days. It's not like you have to ask the fellow in the fancy car at the stoplight for it. (I just lost the readers of this book who were born after 1985. I'm sorry, but not everything is for you.)

On top of this unholy mess, you will sprinkle a teaspoon of dried oregano and a teaspoon of kosher salt. Don't look at me like that - spend the $2 and buy some kosher salt for cooking with, and then always buy the same brand because not all kosher salts have the same amount of salt per measurement. You can Google this if you just got confused, but for now, just go with it, OK?

Crush 10 saltine crackers into crumbs, and add them to the bowl. If you don't have any saltines, a 1/4 cup of store-bought bread-crumbs will work too. In fact, I will buy one of those cardboard tubes of breadcrumbs and just keep them in a dry corner of my pantry just for this dish. They keep forever.

Look in the bowl. It's a mess, isn't it? It's about to get worse. Now, roll up your sleeves, put your hands in the bowl, and knead it together. Imagine you are 4 again, and playing with clay. Let it go through your fingers as you squeeze the mixture. Mix it all together like you are making dough.

When it's all mixed together, you will have a moist mixture, which will seem just a tad too moist. It's fine, except for those of you who just shuddered that I used the word moist twice. (There it goes again!) Using your hands, make four oval-shaped patties, each about 3/4 of an inch thick. Put them on a plate and go wash your hands.

In a large (10-inch or better) cast iron skillet, add a tablespoon of fat - butter is fine here, as is vegetable oil or olive oil or bacon grease - over medium high heat. When the fat is hot, add the steaks and then cook them for about 3 minutes on each side - you may have to turn the heat down if they get too crunchy, but you want a nice crust on each side. When each side is browned and crusty, remove them from the heat and put them on a plate or cooling rack to rest.

Note: They are still likely raw in the middle at this point. That's fine. You ain't done yet.

It's time to make some gravy.

Gravy is the sort of thing that people fret about making, but you need not. It's pretty simple to do; the third time you do it, it will be locked in your memory forever. This is a quick brown "water" gravy, as opposed to a cream gravy like you would put over biscuits or toast.

You can also use this basic brown gravy recipe for putting on your mashed potatoes or rice.

Turn the skillet to medium heat. Don't rinse it out or try to clean it up or anything. There will be some grease and bits of meat in the bottom of the pan. This is right and good, and part of the Lord's plan for the universe. Throw in two tablespoons of butter and, using your whisk, stir it into the drippings until it melts. Then add two tablespoons of flour to this, all the while whisking.

Whisk, whisk, whisk. I'm not precious about kitchen tools, but you need a whisk to make good gravy. And for the love of God, don't try to do this in a nonstick skillet.

When your flour is well mixed into the grease, and you don't have any lumps, add a cup and a half of beef stock to the flour mixture while whisking. You want to get the corners of the skillet while you are at it. Whisk, whisk, whisk.

You don't have to use beef stock here. You could have used water, and I suspect many people do. But if you use beef stock, it just tastes... beefier. Protip: If your liquid is hot when you add it to the flour mixture, it's more likely to be a smoother gravy.

So far, so good. Now we are about to get controversial. Lots of folks just stop here and let the gravy cook for 5 minutes or so, occasionally stirring, allowing the gravy to thicken. And you can - there's nothing wrong with that. But to kick the umami up a notch, squirt in a tablespoon of ketchup, a teaspoon of Worcestershire sauce, and half a teaspoon of onion powder, and whisk to combine it all. Then let it simmer for five minutes to let it thicken somewhat.

Remember those partially cooked patties? We will slide them into the gravy, sort of pushing them around until they are settled in well. Put a lid on the skillet and allow it to simmer for another 15 minutes.

That's almost enough time to make some fancy rice to go along with this.

I call this fancy rice because rice is the first recipe I ever learned - 1 cup of rice, two cups of boiling water, reduce to a simmer, and cover for 18 minutes.

I remember a breakthrough happening in my head when I realized that it wasn't just a recipe but a ratio. Twice as much water as rice, always. You literally cannot mess it up.

I like recipes I cannot mess up.

But, if you want to put a little effort into this, you can make something that tastes dramatically better than plain rice. You can make fancy rice.

You need a cup and a half of white rice to serve four people. Not your Uncle Ben's parboiled rice, jasmine rice, basmati rice, or wild rice, which isn't even rice at all but is instead a sort of grass, but just plain white long grain rice.

You are going to want to rinse your rice. I hear some of you fussing already. OK, fine, you win. You don't have to rinse your rice, but your dinner doesn't have to taste good either.

So, rinse the rice. Put the rice in a medium-sized bowl, and then cover it with water. Swirl the rice in the water and then pour it through a strainer if you have one or a colander lined with a cloth if you don't. Rinsing the starches off the rice improves it dramatically, making it less gummy and sticky. It also makes it cook quicker. It's also just the right way to do it.

Take a medium saucepan (mine is the 3-quart size) and put it over medium heat, add two tablespoons of olive oil (I told you this was fancy), and allow it to warm up. When it's hot, add the rice, which is still damp from being rinsed off, and stir it in the oil. You want to coat the rice in the oil, and the heat will dry the rice, and keep stirring until the rice becomes slightly transparent. It will just take a minute or two.

To the rice, now add three cups of chicken broth. Replacing water with broth is a simple, inexpensive way to dramatically elevate any dish that relies on the water being absorbed, like rice, oatmeal, or, my favorite, grits. But that's another chapter.

If you don't have broth, don't worry - I generally don't either. But you can buy "chicken base," which is just a broth that has had the hound boiled out of it, as my grandmother would have said, and is now a paste you added to water to make a reconstituted broth. You can find chicken base in the grocery store, over where the bouillon cubes are. It keeps in the fridge forever.

Crank up the heat until the broth boils, then turn it to a very low simmer and put the lid on it. Set the timer for 18 minutes. Do not remove the lid. You will be tempted. But don't you do it. In fact, when the timer goes off at 18 minutes, don't even open it then. Just turn off the heat and set the table.

There are lots of variations to this meal. For example, you can slice an onion up fine, then caramelize it in butter for 15 minutes or so and add it to the gravy before reintroducing the steaks. You can do a similar thing with white button mushrooms - slice them fine, sauté them in butter, and then add them to the gravy before you do the steaks. If you are feeling particularly froggy, you can add both onions AND mushrooms.

Some people serve this with mashed potatoes, but as I said, potatoes don't keep well down here, so we only do that at celebrations. When I eat this, I mostly make a mound of rice, which I then cover in the gravy, with the steak on the side. I know some people who put both the steak and the gravy on top of the rice, but then some people will do anything for attention.

Salisbury steak

Ingredients

- 1 pound of ground beef – 73% lean is fine.

- 1/4 cup of crushed crackers or breadcrumbs

- 1 large egg

- 2 teaspoons of ketchup

- 1 teaspoon of Dijon mustard

- 1 teaspoon of dried oregano

- 1 teaspoon of kosher salt

- 1 tablespoon vegetable oil (for the skillet)

In a large bowl, combine all the ingredients, except the oil. Knead with your hands until well combined. Shape the mixture (which will be a little moist) into four patties, around ¾ of an inch thick.

In a cast iron skillet, warm the oil over a medium heat, and then cook the steaks for about three minutes on each side until browned and lightly crusted. You may have to turn down the heat if they get too brown too fast. The patties will still be uncooked inside when you are finished browning them. Add them to the gravy (see below) when it's ready and then simmer for 15 minutes to allow the patties to finish cooking.

Brown quick gravy

Ingredients

- 2 tablespoons butter

- 2 tablespoons all-purpose flour

- 1 1/2 cups beef stock (or 1 ½ cup hot water plus beef base)

Technically optional, but not really:

- 1 tablespoon ketchup

- 1 teaspoon Worcestershire sauce

- 1/2 teaspoon onion powder

In the pan the patties were cooked in, with drippings still in the pan, melt the butter and, then when it's melted, add the flour, and whisk until well combined, and no lumps remain.

Turn down the heat to medium low, and then add the beef stock, whisking well to avoid lumps. Add the remaining ingredients and simmer for 5 minutes to thicken.

Fancy rice

Ingredients

- 1 ½ cups of long grain rice, rinsed

- 2 tablespoons of olive oil

- 3 cups of chicken broth

Rinse the rice, removing the starch, then drain. Heat the olive oil in a saucepan over medium heat, then add the damp rice and sauté until rice is translucent – 2-3 minutes. Add the chicken broth, bring to a boil, reduce to simmer, and then cover and let simmer for 18 minutes. At the end of 18 minutes, turn off the heat and let the pot sit there, unopened, until ready to serve.

6

THE BOX AT THE SIDE OF THE ROAD

It didn't look like much, sitting there on the side of the road, sticking out of a box along side a broken air popper and a lamp with a missing lampshade. But you couldn't fool me – I knew it for what it was.

My brother-in-law was visiting and he had gotten up early and gone for a walk in the neighborhood. When he came back, he told me that a few streets over someone had set a box of trash at the curb.

"And sitting right on top of it all is a cast iron skillet."

I drove over to check it out. It was, in fact, a cast iron skillet; a 10 inch one, to be exact. It wasn't any collectable brand; just a no-name workhorse of a skillet, the sort that used to be in every southern kitchen and still hangs on the wall of mine.

But it had been a long time since somebody loved it. It was filthy and covered in rust. I put it in my shed to "deal with later". And then a few weeks later, a global pandemic happened, and my mind became filled with other things.

But when cleaning out the shed I came across it again and decided it had been neglected long enough.

Cast iron is sacred to me, in a way other skillets are not. They have soul, personality, and character. Perhaps it is all the vibrations in the carbon it has picked up over the years, being present for the family conversations, the supper time arguments, the grunting and poetry of love. In any event, it was time to make things right.

It is true that cast iron cookware requires skill to care for, but it isn't rocket science. It requires a modicum of care, and there are rules to its use, just like there are rules to how to use nonstick.

I ran a sink of hot water and dish soap, and scrubbed it down with a Scotchbrite pad. I scrubbed the grease and the rust off, and when it was done, it was a pale grey with some splotches of rust here and there, but clean. I then poured white vinegar in the pan and scrubbed the rust, adding kosher salt to make a paste.

With cast iron, your two enemies are acid and water. But the dose makes the poison, and first, we must strip it down before we can season it.

After it's clean, I turned the burner of the stove to low heat and then set the skillet on it for 10 minutes or so. I want it dry as can be, and the heat drives the moisture out. While that's happening, I turn the oven on 450 to let it heat up and then get out the vegetable oil.

There is a lot of mythology around seasoning the skillet, but it's just that – myth. All you are going to do is create a thin coating to protect the skillet. And virtually any oil will work. The old folks used lard, because that is what they had, but plain old vegetable oil will work a treat. What we are going to aim for is 4-5 thin coatings. You don't want one thick coating, because it will glob up and get sticky.

OK, now your skillet is on the burner, and dry and scalding hot. Pour a small dot of oil in the skillet – like the size of a quarter, maybe. Then put on an oven mitt and, with a pair of tongs and a folded up paper towel, smear a thin coat of oil over the entire skillet, inside and out. I can't emphasize how little oil will be on the skillet at this point – a thin coating, with no oil remaining when you are done smearing. Your skillet will look the same as it did before, only slightly darker from the oil.

Now put it in the oven upside down and leave it there for 30 minutes. It might smoke a bit – this is not failure. Turn off the smoke detector if you have to. Open a window. It will be worth it.

Using your oven mitt, take it out and repeat the whole process. Small dollop of oil, smear it all over, thin coat, put it back in the oven for 30 more minutes.

Then do it again. And again. And again. Do it at least four times total.

You put the skillet in upside down to keep any oil from pooling. There shouldn't be any oil to pool, if you used as little oil as I told you to, but still – better safe than sorry. The fourth time, just turn the oven off and let it cool, with the skillet in it. And when it cools, you are done.

It's now ready to use. You don't have to be precious with it. Use it to fry bacon, make cornbread, or really to cook anything, although you should probably avoid heavily acidic dishes like spaghetti sauce. And when you are done, use a scrubby pad to clean it with a little soapy water – the no soap thing is another myth – and then dry it off by putting it over low heat for a minute or two to drive the moisture out, then wipe it down with a few drops of oil.

And that's it. Using it continues to season it naturally and drying it and wiping it with oil protects it. Keep it dry and it will, properly treated, outlast the kitchen in which it is stored. I do not, however, recommend storing it in a box at the end of the driveway.

7

A POOR MAN'S FEAST

I have never known a life that didn't include beans. White beans, butter beans, green beans, kidney beans, black-eyed peas (which is really a bean), purple hull peas (also a bean), and, of course, pinto beans – if it was a bean, we ate it.

Bean night was a thrill in my house growing up - which was a good thing because it happened pretty often. You could stretch just a little meat to feed lots of people, and even the meat was optional if you had some bacon grease in the fridge for seasoning.

I once asked my mom why we were having beans and cornbread again. Didn't we have beans and cornbread on Monday night?

No, she told me. We had cornbread and beans on Monday. Tonight, we were having beans and cornbread.

Oh.

I don't know if you have beans in your pantry, but you should. Hell, I don't know if you even have a pantry - maybe you are the sort of person who buys their food fresh every day from the farmer's market and then lightly sautés it in free-range shade-grown organic butter. But I don't know anything about what it is to live like that.

Working folks have generally always had a pantry if they could afford to, even if it wasn't called that. It's just some amount of food put by for when times are harder than they are now. Boundless optimism that things will always improve is the stuff of the middle class, who have enough margin in their lives to afford such notions.

But for folks who live closer to the bone, the knowledge that fortune is a fickle beast is bred into us. You never know when the work might dry up, your car might need an emergency repair, or a global pandemic comes along and stays around for 30 months or so. Sometimes you have more, and sometimes you have less. But in all circumstances, fortune favors the prepared.

When I go to the grocery store for practically any purpose, I have a list of things I look for to see if they are cheap that day, and if they are, they go in the pantry.

Things like butter, salt, coffee, ground beef, and ham. And beans. Always beans. You should, I am convinced, always have some dried beans in your pantry. Beans are cheap – a pound of pintos is roughly a dollar, give or take, and will feed six people. Four if they are hungry. They keep for ages. They are an excellent source of protein. And they taste amazing.

You were probably with me up until that last sentence. But they do – correctly seasoned, like these are, beans and cornbread are a miracle food that has kept many a working person nourished and fed and happy. They are, done right, a poor man's feast.

When it comes to the holidays, some families are turkey folks, and some are ham folks. We are firmly on team ham. Turkey is alright for Thanksgiving, but all religious holidays involve ham. I don't know how that happened, but I don't make the rules.

The best part of ham for Christmas and Easter is the leftover ham, which is suitable for sandwiches and breakfast meat.

And then there is that bone. You still have a nice bone and some scraps of meat, fat, and skin when it's all said and done. Not a lot in our house, because we love some damn ham, but some. For argument's sake, let's say that there is about a half-pound of leftover meat, skin, and fat, plus the bone. I will stick all that in a freezer bag and put it in the freezer if I don't have any immediate plans. But I usually do.

Regardless, before too much time has passed by, I will have a day when it's cold and gray outside. That day is often a weekend when there is too much month at the end of the money. The combination of the grayness and the lack of desire to spend money means it's time to make beans and cornbread.

Take a pound of pinto beans and pour them on a cookie sheet, looking for rocks and dirt. Next, you pick through them with your fingers, shifting them around until you make sure the beans are clean. This is a meditative action, this sifting for stone, and is probably less necessary than it once was, bean milling being a more efficient process these days. But my belief in the depravity of man is reinforced when I skip this step, having trusted the bean companies to do their job well, to only be met with inevitable disappointment.

Put your clean, sorted beans in a large pot and add cold water until it covers the top of the beans by about two inches. They need to soak in the water for a few hours, and the soaking works better if you stir the soaking beans every so often to ensure water and oxygen get everywhere.

Now, you don't have to do this – the soaking, I mean - no matter what you saw on the Internet. But they taste better if you do, and spend less time actually cooking over heat. The fresher your beans, the less essential the soaking is, but dried beans look the same whether six months or six years old, and beans will give you trust issues, so I always soak them. But don't soak them overnight, as some folks do, or they will break down too much. Four hours is plenty, two is sufficient, and in a pinch, again, none is probably acceptable.

When they are done soaking, pour the water off the beans, and then put more cold water in the bean pot, again about two inches over the beans. Don't drown them – this isn't soup, and it isn't mush; this is beans. Put your ham bone and ham scraps, including the skin and fat, in the pot too. Don't worry too much if the water doesn't cover every little bit of the bone. Turn the heat to high.

As an aside – some folks are already panicking at the mention of ham skin going in this. Just cut it into small pieces and go with it. Most of the fat and collagen will dissolve and turn into flavor. You shouldn't be afraid of food. Well, except maybe for that frozen burrito thing they sell at the gas station. I know that there are people for whom that is all they can get, and I hear that. But it's still a little scary, all the same.

While waiting for the water to boil for your beans, get the rest of your ingredients ready. You need a small onion, maybe the size of a doorknob. I like a sweet yellow onion for this, but I suspect any onion is better than no onion. If times are tough, a heavy dose of onion powder will beat a poke in the eye with a stick, but I imagine most things do. Peel your onion, chop off the ends and then cut it into long strips from pole to pole.

Peel a large clove of garlic. If the garlic you have is puny, add two. You shouldn't be afraid of garlic, either. Put the onions and the whole clove of garlic in the water with the beans and add ½ a tablespoon of salt and ½ a tablespoon of sugar.

I admit that sugar and garlic are controversial choices and ones I did not grow up with but instead learned from the kitchen of others. However, they dramatically elevate the dish.

The beans will probably need another ½ tablespoon of salt later in the cooking, but a lot depends on how salty the ham is, and you won't know for a while. As to salt, it's always easier to add than to take it out.

After your beans get to a rolling boil, you want to back off to a medium or low – whatever it takes to do a slow boil, just a bit more than a simmer. With your pot covered, you want this to go on for about an hour, but stir the beans every 10-15 minutes. If you are doing other things, just do it as you pass through the kitchen – no need to set a timer or anything.

After your hour passes, turn it lower to a simmer and stir every so often. You will also need to make sure you don't boil all your liquid away. I keep a glass of water on the counter by the stove when I'm making beans, and I add a bit from time to time, always making sure to not drown them. But, again, this isn't soup. You want to keep an inch, no more than two, of water over the top of the beans.

Two hours in, check for salt, and most likely, add another half tablespoon. This is one of the danger points – too much salt makes them not fit to eat. By now, the broth is brown and has a filmy appearance as the meat and marrow dissolve into the bean juice and make something amazing.

I don't know how long this dish takes to make – there are a lot of variables. Fresher beans cook faster than older beans, and temperature settings like High and Medium are subjective. And I haven't ever cooked on your stove. But somewhere between two and a half and three hours, take a couple of beans out and mash them between your fingers. If the bean splits in two, keep cooking. But a perfect bean will be slightly firm and mash evenly between your fingers. Think of the difference between a raw potato and a baked potato. We are going for a baked potato here. If nobody is looking, you can eat a few and see how they taste. The meat will, by this time, have fallen off the bone and left it clean.

This is when you turn the heat down to the lowest possible setting and put a lid on it, so it stays warm because now it's time to make cornbread.

If there is food that stirs strong opinions here in the Southland, it's cornbread. Although, in our defense, it's a highly personal food that fills a lot of roles. Cornbread can be the backbone of an otherwise skimpy supper, the thing you use to push the food on your fork, the heart of a good dressing, or even. when crumbled in a glass of buttermilk, dessert.

But the biggest problem, I think, comes about because people who have only eaten cornbread during the holidays at other people's houses don't know how easy it is to make. So, they get scared and end up using a mix to make it, and lots of mixes have loads of sugar in them.

There is a place for cornbread that contains sugar and flour. I'm tempted to be cheeky here and say that place is the trash can, but I always put sugar and flour in my corn muffins, which I cover elsewhere in these pages. But you want a stouter, savory bread for beans and cornbread.

Before we get started on this cornbread, we need to talk about skillets. Specifically, yours, and whether it's cast iron or whether it's wrong. To do cornbread the right way, you really need an 8 to 10-inch well-seasoned cast-iron skillet. But maybe you are not at a place in your life where someone loves you enough to have given you a cast iron skillet and taught you how to care for it. In that case, you could use a 9-inch cake pan until things change for you, but cornbread will crust up better in a cast-iron skillet. Don't shoot the messenger.

Turn your oven to 450 degrees and allow it to heat up. Meanwhile, put 2 tablespoons of butter in your skillet and set it in the heating oven to melt. I said butter, but you could also use margarine or bacon drippings here. Honestly, they all work about the same, and which one I use is more a function of budget and availability than anything else. Mostly, I use butter because it's easy to measure, and we don't keep margarine in the house.

While the butter is melting in the oven, it's time to mix the batter. Again, this moves fast, so pay attention.

It all starts with the cornmeal. White cornmeal is traditional here, but yellow is easier to get, and I can't tell a taste difference. I can tell you that you can fancy this up by using a stone-ground meal here, but it's still good if you use a generic yellow meal from the grocery store. Put a cup of the meal in a mixing bowl, and add a teaspoon of baking powder and half a teaspoon of salt in with it. Stir well until it is all incorporated. (That means mixed up well).

Some people put more baking powder than this in their cornbread, the idea being that it will make the bread rise more, but this isn't a cake - I like a denser bread. But you can, if you want, even double this amount of baking powder and still be okay.

Having mixed the dry ingredients, pour in a cup of buttermilk. If you don't have any buttermilk, you can make do by adding two tablespoons of lemon juice to a cup of milk and letting it sit out for about 15 minutes. You really just need an acid to react to the baking powder.

But really, you ought to have buttermilk. It keeps a long time in your fridge - much longer than the use-by date would have you believe - and also freezes well. If you don't have any other use for buttermilk, you can always buy powdered buttermilk in the baking aisle of your store, which keeps forever.

On top of the buttermilk, crack a large egg. With a fork, mix the contents of the mixing bowl - meal, salt, baking powder, buttermilk, and egg - together well, making a thick batter with an even consistency. It's easy to over-mix this, but you will be fine if you use a fork and not a mixer. Again, we are not making a cake.

Now, remove the skillet from the oven (be careful, it's hot!), swirl the melted butter all over the skillet to coat the bottom, and then pour the melted butter into the batter. Stir the batter once or twice to mix the butter in, then pour the batter into the skillet. Jiggle the skillet to distribute the batter evenly. Then slide it back in the oven and feel morally superior about your life choices.

It will be done when it's done, as my momma used to say, but more helpful is to know that when it's done: It will be golden brown on top, and the sides of the bread will have pulled away from the sides of the skillet, and a knife inserted in the middle of the cornbread will come out clean. An 8-inch cast-iron skillet will take about 20 minutes, and a 10-inch one will take around 17.

In our house, we just cut it into wedges and serve it from the skillet. When we were growing up, momma would invert it on a plate and serve it upside down, which bothered me in ways I cannot fully describe. But you do you.

This is a basic, make 30 minutes before supper, all-purpose cornbread. This is also good dressing cornbread, if you are making chicken and dressing, but you will want to make it the day before so it can dry out for that. You can fancy this up by adding a half cup of shredded cheese, a handful of frozen corn kernels, or a small drained can of green chiles to the batter before cooking. But don't go too close to the sun here: This is meant to be simple food.

Serving Instructions

When you plate this meal, make sure you put some meat pieces in each serving. The meat is very much part of this dish, as is the cornbread. I like it in a bowl with lots of broth to sop up with my cornbread, but some folk like it on a plate.

Either way, I am fond of putting some chow-chow relish on it, but my Dad always put pepper sauce on his. I knew one guy in the Marines that put ketchup on his beans – I never did trust that guy. Let your conscience be your guide.

Pintos and ham

Ingredients

- 1 pound of pinto beans

- ½ pound leftover ham, plus ham bone.

- Small yellow onion

- 1-2 large cloves of garlic

- ½ tablespoon of salt

- ½ tablespoon of sugar

Sort and clean your beans, then soak in cold water for at least four hours, stirring occasionally. Then drain, and cover again with cold water

Southern cornbread

Ingredients

- 1 cup cornmeal, either yellow or white

- 1 tsp baking powder

- 1/2 tsp salt

- 1 cup buttermilk (See narrative for alternatives.)

- 1 large egg

- 2 TBS butter or margarine

- 1 8 to 10-inch well-seasoned cast iron skillet or cake pan

- 1 cup cornmeal, either yellow or white

- 1 tsp baking powder

- 1/2 tsp salt

- 1 cup buttermilk

- 1 large egg

- 2 tablespoons of butter or margarine

- 1 8 to 10-inch well-seasoned cast-iron skillet or, if your life is not going well, a cake pan

Preheat the oven to 450. Put butter in a cast-iron skillet and then put the skillet in the oven to melt.

Mix the dry ingredients in a bowl and then add the egg and buttermilk to the dry stuff and mix with a spoon until the batter has an even consistency. Remove the skillet (be careful, it's hot!), swirl the melted butter all over the skillet, then pour the melted butter into the batter.

Stir the batter once to incorporate the butter, then pour the batter into the skillet, and jiggle it so the batter is evenly distributed.

Put it in the oven until it's done: it will be golden brown on top, the sides will pull away from the side of the skillet, and a knife blade comes out dry from the center. For an 8-inch skillet, this takes about 20 minutes; a 10-inch one, about 17.

8

MR. TOMMY'S BUTT

E very holiday has its rituals and its food.

There are gifts, chocolate fudge, and a decorated tree at Christmas. Thanksgiving is a huge meal with a turkey and dressing and Aunt Louise's cranberry sauce. On the Fourth of July there's hot dogs and fireworks. And, of course, on Labor Day, there was Mr. Tommy's butt.

Mr. Tommy was an older man who was our state representative, and his barbecue prowess was well known. Every year, he would sell barbecued pork butts as a fundraiser for the Lion's Club, a fine organization of which he was a proud and lifetime member.

Before we go much further in this, I need to get some terms out of the way. In this volume, we will use the word barbecue the correct way, because we are not damned heathens. I shall never forget the time when some folks from California invited me to their house because they were going to barbecue. When I got there, they handed me a hot dog. I considered suit for false advertising.

Then there were the people from England who were very excited and wanted to show me the new barbecue they had just bought.

"Pulled pork, or ribs"? I asked.

With a look of confusion, they took me outside to show me their new gas grill.

Welp. Jesus loves these people and knows I'm trying to.

No, where I come from, barbecue is neither an event nor an appliance. It is, rather, a method of cooking - namely, a long, slow, dry heat that breaks down the connective tissues of tougher cuts of meat. It is somewhat appliance agnostic. One can make perfectly acceptable barbecue on a gas grill or in an oven in the house, and some folks even use a crock pot. I bet that, as we speak, right now on TikTok somebody is trying to go viral using an InstaPot. But the canonical method involves charcoal.

And while we are on the subject: Barbecue is an incredibly regionally diverse cooking method. For example, the barbecue in Memphis (most properly pork spare ribs, done over charcoal with a dry rub and no sauce) is significantly different than the barbecue one finds in Dallas, where they use beef brisket. Then there is North Carolina, where, as you get closer to the coast, they abandon tomatoes and bring pepper sauce into the mix. And none of them have any affinity with the barbecue in South Carolina, where they cook pork but then throw all the rules out entirely and use a mustard sauce.

But it is always long, slow, and as close as we come in these homogenized times to having a genuine regional cuisine. And in the minds of my people, barbecue was always smoked pork butts like Mr. Tommy did every year.

This is simple, inexpensive food made by people with more time than money. Pork butts are just the top of the pig's shoulder and have nothing to do with anybody's posterior, either the pig's or Mr. Tommy's. And, importantly to this discussion, they are a pretty inexpensive cut of meat. You will probably find they are about 5-6 pounds and will be sold with the skin off. Some stores will call them "Boston Butts." Your butcher will help you out here.

Mr. Tommy had a complicated setup involving an oil drum split in half and racks welded in, but as we are just doing one at a time, I just use the same charcoal grill I would use to cook steaks on. Some people spend thousands of dollars on their barbecue setup. You need not be one of those people. For less than $150 of kit, you can make the best pork butt in the world. Or at least the best pork butt in your world.

People who have never made pulled pork before get scared sometimes. There is no need. This is an incredibly forgiving technique. People have done this for generations with little to no equipment. You can do this.

You need a charcoal grill. It can be the $50 one from the hardware store, because as long as it has a damper on the lid and another on the bottom, it will work. If you spent a lot of money on your grill, it might have a thermometer in the lid. If you spent even more money, that thermometer might be accurate. Neither of those things are true in my case, so I bought two digital thermometers with probes. They are not fancy - I think I paid less than $20 apiece for them online, and they have tons of uses beyond barbecue. The Mr. Tommy's of the world did not cook to temperature but to time, smell, and taste. The rest of us cheat and use thermometers.

One thermometer will measure the ambient temperature inside the grill - we want it to stay around 250 degrees. The other will be stuck in the fleshiest part of the butt itself, and eventually, we want that to hit 200 degrees. But we have some work to do first.

Plain charcoal is fine. And I do mean plain. Don't get the stuff with lighter fluid built in. It's an abomination. You also need some wood for smoking, but you don't need a lot. Pretty much any hardwood will do here. The wood of fruit trees like cherry or apple imparts a flavor some folks like, and others swear by hickory or oak. My people tended to use pecan, but that was mostly because we had so much of it around. Three or four pieces of hardwood about the size of a tennis ball is plenty.

If you live in town and don't have a friend with a wood-burning fireplace, I saw a bag of wood chunks for sale the last time I was at the grocery store, over near the charcoal. You want chunks, not chips.

While you are at the store, get something like an 8x8 aluminum foil pan. We will use that as a drip pan to keep the butt moist and clean up easier. Also, if you don't have one, get a clean pistol grip spray bottle, like the kind window cleaner comes in.

The butt will have one side with a lot of fat on it and the other doesn't. From now on, we will call the side with the fat "the top." People who win competitions at this call it "The Fat Cap". But it's just the top.

Put the butt on a cutting board, and using a sharp knife, score a series of hash marks (like drawing a Tic Tac Toe symbol) in the fat. Wipe it dry with a paper towel, salt and pepper each side generously, and then rub the whole thing down with your rub mixture. People get precious about their pork rubs, but for a pork butt, I keep it simple and just use a mix of paprika, onion powder, and sugar.

Some folks cover their butts in mustard to get the rub to stay on, but I find it's not really a problem, and it's just one more step. We just pour the rub on and then, using our hands, rub it all over the butt, allowing it to get deep in the crevices and cracks. Now, cover it loosely with a towel and set it on the counter to rest while you go get the grill ready.

Open the dampers on your grill, both on the bottom and on top, to wide open. In the beginning, we want all the air there is. Next, in the bottom of the grill, where you put the charcoal, put your 8x8 pan in the middle, fill it half full of water, and surround it with charcoal on three sides, making a sort of horseshoe around the pan. Next, take your three chunks of hardwood and put them on top of one end of the horseshoe of charcoal.

Now we are ready to start. I put a handful of briquettes in a charcoal chimney and light them using a wad of newspaper. After ten minutes or so, I pour them on the end of the charcoal horseshoe where the chunks of hardwood are.

The theory is that the few pieces of charcoal we lit will ignite the adjacent pieces around the horseshoe for the six hours or so this will take. This will mean less messing around with the grill and less moving things, thus less chance of messing things up. Also, the chunks of wood should be at the same end of the horseshoe as the lit briquettes because most of the benefit from the smoke comes early in the process.

Replace the grill grate. If you are like me, you may have to adjust the mountain of coals and wood you just made to get everything to fit. Using one of your probe thermometers, put the probe on the grill surface over the pan of water (not the fire!), then place the lid on the grill.

You want the temperature to get up to about 275. We will be cooking much lower than that, but when you put the butt on the grill, it will drop the temperature dramatically. This gives us a bit of a head start.

It will most likely take somewhere around 45 minutes to hit 275 degrees. When it gets close, get your butt and insert the probe from the other thermometer in the meatiest part of the butt. Set it over the pan of water, fat side up, and then put the lid on. You probably lost at least 100 degrees. Keep an eye on the ambient thermometer - the goal is to get back up to 225. It will probably take at least 30 minutes for this to happen.

While waiting on that, fill your spray bottle halfway full of Apple Cider vinegar and then the rest of the way with water. Every hour from now on, you will spray the butt with a spray of the vinegar water mix.

When it hits 225, close the dampers about halfway. More air equals more heat. Less air equals less heat. For the next six hours or so, you need to keep an eye on the ambient temperature, trying your best to keep it between 225 and 250. And once an hour, take the lid off and spray it with the vinegar mixture.

This sounds like a lot of work, but it's really about 15 minutes of active bother over six hours or so. Barbecue is a reflective art - you can't cram a thing like this like you could 11th-grade chemistry exam. It takes the time it takes. Much like cooking beans, you will enjoy it more by just giving yourself over to the process.

The first goal is to get the internal thermometer to 165 degrees. At that point, your butt is technically "done," as in, it's not raw. You could remove it at this point and slice it for sandwiches, say. But it needs to get up to 200 degrees before it's ready to be pulled. At 200 degrees, the connective tissue and collagen have dissolved to such a degree that it will literally fall apart. Then, and only then, is it ready.

Now, honesty compels me to tell you that some people remove the butt from the grill at this point. They wrap it in aluminum foil and, after reinserting the thermometer probe, put it in a 300-degree oven and allow it to go the rest of the way to 200 degrees in the oven, inside, where the beer and the air conditioner are.

I get that, but I don't do that myself. I just leave it on the grill, just like it is, spraying it every so often, watching the temperature creep slowly up to 200 degrees. How fast this takes depends on a lot of things, including the outside temperature, the humidity, and so on.

We will fast forward now to when your butt hits 200 degrees, probably about six hours after you first put your butt on the grill. You have been victorious! Shout "hell yeah," give yourself a high five, and then remove the butt to a plate and wrap it in aluminum foil. If you will be eating in the next hour or so, I would let it rest on the counter. If it will be longer than an hour, let it rest in an insulated dry cooler, so it stays warm. In any event, it needs to rest for at least half an hour.

Serving it is as easy as can be. You shred (or "pull") the pork after it has rested by using two forks and pulling it apart into, well, shreds. Done well, there will be pieces of crispy fat, pieces of the bark or crust, and pieces of tender pork well distributed throughout.

In any fine barbecue establishment, you will be offered a "pulled pork plate", which will probably involve a mound of pulled pork, baked beans, slaw, and a piece of buttery Texas toast. There is nothing wrong with this. In fact, there is much that is right with it.

I, personally, love a good pulled pork sandwich, however. I take pulled pork, place about two ounces of it on cheap hamburger buns, with a dollop of cheap barbecue sauce (something tomato based with both sugar and vinegar in it is what I grew up on, but use what tastes god to you) and a mayonnaise and vinegar slaw on top of it. Served with watermelon in season and crinkle-cut French fries anytime, it is enough to burn a permanent smile into the memory of a 10-year-old boy.

After having made a pulled pork butt, you will have leftover butt rub. That is normal. You can put it in a mason jar with a lid on it and stick it in the pantry with your other spices for next time. Or, you can make butt-rubbed potatoes.

When you remove the butt from your grill, and it's resting, carefully remove the pan of water from your grill and set it aside. With a spatula or something, pull all of the remaining briquettes into the center of the grill, and open all the dampers. Put the lid back on the grill. You want it to get roaring hot under there.

You will need one fist-sized russet potato per person for this. Scrub it clean under running water and remove any eyes and bad spots with a sharp knife. Then put them in a pan, cover with water, and bring it to a boil for about 8 minutes - until a knife can be inserted, but before they become crumbly. Remove them from the water and dry them off.

(You can absolutely do the preceding in advance and let them cool on the counter. I often do this in the boring part of the butt cooking, where I am waiting for it to hit an internal temperature of 200 degrees. It also makes the next part easier if they are not boiling hot).

Slice them lengthwise in half and then into thirds, so you end up with six huge potato wedges. Set them on a baking sheet, drizzle them with olive oil, and then, using your fingers, massage the oil into them, so they are covered with it. Remember that your potatoes are somewhat tender at this point and can't handle a lot of rough handling. Be gentle. That is good advice most days, come to think of it.

Coat them liberally on all sides with kosher salt and the leftover barbecue rub, and then put them on the grill over the heap of coals. Cover with the lid and turn them every few minutes until they are crispy and have lovely grill marks. People love these, and they look fancy and take almost no effort.

Butt rub

Ingredients

- 1.5 cups of paprika

- ¾ cup of granulated sugar

- 4 tablespoons of onion powder

Put all three ingredients in a pint mason jar, close the lid, and shake well. You can keep the leftovers for six months or so, but it never sticks around that long in my house.

Pulled pork butt

Ingredients

- 5-6 pound pork butt

- Butt rub

- Salt

- Pepper

- Apple cider vinegar

Special equipment
- A charcoal grill, with lid

- 2 thermometers with cable probes

- 8x8(ish) disposable aluminum pan

- Charcoal

- Lumps of hardwood, canonically pecan, but feel free to experiment. Do NOT use conifer wood (pine, fir, cedar, etc)

- A pistol grip sprayer

After removing the grate, insert the 8x8 aluminum pan in the base of the charcoal grill. Fill it half full of water. Surround the pan on three sides with charcoal, 2-3 pieces deep, so they all touch another piece. At one end of the resulting U, place 2-3 small pieces of pecan (or other wood – see note) on top of the charcoal.

Using a charcoal chimney, light 4-5 pieces of charcoal and get them well established – perhaps 10 minutes. Using tongs, place them at the end of the U that has the pecan wood, so they will light the unlit wood. (See note for further explanation).

Replace the grate, open the dampers wide open, and cover the grill. Use one of the remote probe thermometers to monitor the heat over the pan of water. This is your "ambient" heat. Your goal is to preheat the grill to an ambient heat of 275.

While it's preheating, dry the pork butt, score the side with the layer of fat on it perhaps ½ inch deep in a hash pattern (like Tic Tac Toe), and then salt and pepper all sides. Then rub a generous coating of butt rub on all sides. Allow to sit at room temperature until the grill reaches an ambient temp of 275 degrees.

When the grill reaches 275, place the butt over the pan of water (but not on top of the probe – move the probe toward the side of the grill without charcoal.) Insert the other probe in the fleshiest part of the butt. This is your "internal" temp, and your goal is 200.

When the ambient temp reaches 220 or so, close the damper to about half, and then open or close it over the next few hours to keep your ambient temp between 200 and 250. (See note for more explanation on this). Each hour, remove the lid and mist the butt with a 50/50 mixture of cider vinegar and water.

When internal temp hits 200, remove from the grill, and rest for at least half an hour. Pull into pieces with two forks and serve to suit.

9

TWENTY-FIVE DOLLAR GRITS

In my twenties, I was trying to get ahead and went to work as an insurance sales associate. They told me the key was to sell insurance to people who have a lot of money. I didn't know anybody who had a lot of money. But I worked my networks, and people were kind, and slowly I got introduced to good potential customers.

One of them was a man named Dan, who lived in an affluent suburb of Memphis. Dan was a CPA and had the potential to not only be a good customer himself, but he knew a lot of business owners who also stood to be good potential customers. My sales manager told me I should "cultivate the relationship" by taking him to lunch.

I told Dan I wanted to take him out to eat at his favorite restaurant. It turns out Dan loved Italian food.

My experience of Italian food in 1995 was limited to spaghetti, things that came from Pizza Hut, and that master of the Italian kitchen, Chef Boyardee.

"I love Italian," I told him.

We went to this elegant restaurant that had white tablecloths. Dan ordered a basket of garlic knots. We looked over the menu. I recognized the spaghetti and meatballs and could use context clues to figure out what pumpkin ravioli was. Pizza was nowhere to be seen.

Being no dummy, I asked Dan what was good.

"Their polenta is amazing," he said. "Do you like polenta?"

These days, I would excuse myself, go to the bathroom, and use my phone to Google, "What is polenta?".

Alas, this was 1995.

"I love polenta," I told him.

We ordered polenta with sausage and peppers. I at least knew what sausage and peppers were.

When the order came, we ate and talked about the services I could offer and why it made sense for him to do business with me. He agreed, and ultimately, we worked together for several years. I was on point that day.

Which is amazing, because the whole time I was eating lunch, all I could think about is that I had just spent $50 on two plates of gad-danged grits and spaghetti sauce.

Now, before the spirit of some Italian grandma rises up from the grave and haunts me forever, I am compelled to mention that grits and polenta are not the same things. There are two main differences, one being that grits are most properly made from ground white corn, and polenta is made from ground yellow corn, so there is a slightly different flavor profile. The other main difference is that the polenta comes in a box that said "polenta" on it.

In practice, they are similar enough to be largely interchangeable. Grits and polenta are much closer than collards and kale, which are also interchangeable.

If ever there was an example of my adage that "Normal is just another word for whatever you are used to," it's grits. And if you can do it to a bowl of grits, I assure you somebody has.

Growing up, grits were for breakfast. Mom liked them because the preparation was simple, it was filling, and it was as cheap as could be. One thing momma didn't like about grits, unfortunately, was the grits themselves: She tended to prefer Cream of Wheat but never managed to convert us. But she grew up traveling around the country with my grandfather, who was in the Navy, so one has to make allowances.

When visiting our neighbors, Monty and Doc, I would sometimes eat fried grits for lunch. This was simply leftover grits poured into a loaf pan, then cooled in the refrigerator until firm. They would then be sliced into ¾-inch thick slabs that were then dredged through a 50-50 mixture of flour and cornmeal and then fried in bacon grease, making an ersatz fried polenta. If bacon grease is not your thing, you could use canola or corn oil or, if you insist, olive oil. You could even use avocado oil, but if you did, I wouldn't tell anyone about it.

Fried grits is lovely by itself or served with a drizzle of pancake syrup or sorghum molasses on it. The texture and sweetness go well together. You can also serve it for supper with a red sauce, such as we will discuss later.

But that meal with Dan changed my view of grits forever, giving me language for experimentation I had not previously had. It was, in terms of my cooking, one of my formative meals. Because it helped me see, perhaps for the first time, how interconnected all our food paths were. It's like the blinders were off. The cooking world was my oyster.

The cooking world does not always do a good job bringing other people into the fold. There are gatekeepers who want to ensure that the secrets are kept, that only the right people get in, and that only the proper people get credit.

Some of this gatekeeping is innocence – The only way I knew to do a thing was the way I had been taught, so of course, it seemed like the right way to me. And we cannot teach what we do not know. I would have told you I did not know how to make a bechamel sauce in 1995.

But some of it is also exploitation. We now know that many Southern standards are recipes and innovations developed by enslaved people who were prevented from learning to write and read. The white people who did write them down and then shared them with the world were the ones credited with the recipe.

It turns out that bechamel sauce was milk gravy, the same as we had for breakfast over biscuits my whole life, but without any seasoning to it. Aoli is just mayonnaise with stuff in it. Pancetta is expensive bacon. When Ms. Bessie made mac and cheese in the oven for the church potluck, she made a mornay sauce, despite never having heard the term.

My life would never be the same.

These days, I eat grits more often at suppertime than I do for breakfast, and when I make them, I often make them with sausage and peppers. Because I usually make these as a weeknight meal, I take some liberties to speed things up, but you can have this on the table in about 20 minutes.

You will need some grits. White is traditional, and regular people eat just regular grits. However, there are artisanal, stone-ground grits to be had out there – just be aware they take about twice as long to cook. But for our purposes, some white grits – even the quick-cooking grits, like I do in this recipe - will do on a weeknight. We don't speak of instant grits or anything that comes in an individual serving packet or has extra flavors added.

You will need a liquid. At its most basic, you can use water, and many people do, but milk is a fine choice too. But if you are going to the trouble to make them for supper, try chicken stock instead. So, in this recipe, we will use both chicken stock and milk.

And since I believe in the power of cheese, thanks to the PSA advertisements from the 80s, I would add some cheese. Now, any cheese will do – cheddar (my preference), cream cheese, Velveeta, American – just whatever you have laying around. But honestly, I use cheese grits like this as an opportunity to use up little bits of cheese I might have lurking in the cheese drawer in the fridge.

Here's how I make my version of that meal Dan and I ate 25 years ago today.

I'd put 4 cups of chicken broth in a heavy saucepan, heat it to a boil, and then bring it down to a simmer. Now, if you don't have chicken broth on hand, you can use something like chicken base or some chicken bouillon cubes instead. The point is that any of that will be better than just water.

Now that it's simmering, slowly add 1 cup of quick-cooking grits while you whisk them in. If you just dump them in, it will clump up. Instead, do it slowly, stirring the broth as you slowly shake the grits into the pot. When they are all in, add ¾ of a teaspoon of salt, give the mixture a final stir for luck, and then put the lid on the pot, turn it down to low, and let them simmer for a good 10 minutes or so, until they thicken. You will want to stir them at least twice during this time, so they don't stick.

You could stop now and have a fine bowl of grits, but we can keep going and make them extraordinary. Let's add a tablespoon of butter (I use salted butter here because it's what I always have, but unsalted would work too), and a cup to a cup and a half (let your conscience be your guide) of a good sharp shredded Cheddar cheese, the sharper the better. Just stir it in a bit at a time, and watch it melt. This will thicken the grits a bit, especially if you use pre-shredded cheese (it's a weeknight, so you are forgiven), which is coated in cornstarch and thus has a thickening effect on everything. You then will thin it down with about quarter of a cup of whole milk, or if you are feeling festive, half and half or whipping cream.

This serves three people if you do it as a main dish or about six as a side, but you can double it easily. I'd serve it in bowls and sprinkle the top with freshly ground black pepper. Hide the sugar bowl because some folks have never had good grits before and will be tempted to put sugar on them out of habit.

Another cooking revelation for me was coming to the understanding that most "complicated" dishes are just multiple uncomplicated dishes. You just made cheese grits, which are amazing and something you can serve without shame to anyone.

The meal I had with Dan was Italian sausage and peppers in a red sauce, over the grits, errr, polenta. It's still a meal I love, and every time I make it, I feel a little nostalgic for that naive kid who bought lunch for a rich man.

I use a 12-inch cast iron skillet for this. Some folks say you should never use a cast iron skillet for tomato-based dishes because of the acid, but those are people who are afraid of their cast iron and who have pans that are unseasoned. An enameled braiser would also work, or a large sauté pan. You could make it in a saucepan if that's all you have, but it works faster in a shallow, wider dish.

Add two tablespoons of olive oil to your skillet, set it over medium heat, and let it heat up. While it's warming up, take 4 Italian sausage links, rough chop them into small pieces, and add them to the skillet. Alternatively, crumble a pound of bulk sausage into the skillet. For some reason, it seems like one or the other of them is always on sale where I shop, so that's what I use that week.

While it's browning, slice two bell peppers - I usually do one red and one green, because I'm fancy like that - into fine strips and slice a sweet onion the same way. Then, periodically stir the sausage, so it browns evenly. This will take about five minutes.

When the sausage is done, remove it with a slotted spoon and put it on some paper towels to drain. Add the peppers and onion to the fat in the pan, and sauté them until they begin to break down and the onions get translucent - perhaps another five minutes or so.

You need some garlic. This is such an individual choice - I love garlic, and so add 3-5 cloves. But I think it needs at least two. Just peel and dice them and add the garlic after the peppers have broken down, and then sauté them in the mixture for another minute or so. You want to really smell the garlic. But you must be careful here because burnt garlic will taste bitter, and nobody wants that.

When the garlic is fragrant, stir in a couple of teaspoons of dried oregano, and stir it in well. This released a fantastic smell. Then, open a large 28-ounce can of crushed tomatoes, pour them (undrained) over the peppers, and add the cooked sausage back to the mix. Stir it well for luck, then reduce the heat and cover the pan. Let it all simmer for 20 minutes or so.

So far, you haven't added any salt or pepper - I would taste it now and see if it needs it - I find it often doesn't, depending on the sweetness of the peppers and so on. But you do you.

Another thing that I have learned about food is how much presentation matters to the experience. If I'm in a rush to put food on the table, I will put the grits in one serving bowl, the sauce in another, and just plop them on the table and let people serve themselves. Honesty compels me to tell you that on such nights, we generally eat them out of a bowl, with the contents of the green sprinkle cheese can shaken on top for good measure.

But if we have company, I will put the plates in the stove at 170 degrees for the last 15 minutes or so that everything is cooking. Then, I will take a warmed plate and put a cup of cheese grits in the middle. Then, using a large spoon, take up a scoop of the sausage and peppers and put them in the middle, using the base of the spoon to push the grits out from the center. This will leave a pile of grits with sauce in the middle, much like mashed potatoes have gravy in the middle.

Finish it off by sprinkling grated parmesan on top, and you now have a $25 plate of grits.

Cheese grits

Ingredients

- 4 cups of chicken stock

- 1 cup of quick cooking grits

- 1.5 cups of sharp cheddar cheese, shredded

- ¼ cup of half and half or whole milk or heavy cream

- 1 tablespoon of butter

- ¼ teaspoon of salt

Bring the chicken stock to a boil in a large saucepan, then reduce to a simmer. Slowly stir in the grits, reduce the heat to a simmer, and cover the pan. Stir occasionally until the stock is absorbed – 10 minutes or so. Stir in remaining ingredients and allow the cheese to melt.

Sausage and peppers

Ingredients
- 2 tablespoons olive oil

- a pound of Italian sausage

- 2 bell peppers, one red, one green, cut into long strips.

- 1 yellow onion, cut into long strips

- 3 cloves of garlic, minced

- 2 teaspoons of crushed oregano

- 28 oz can of crushed tomatoes

- salt and pepper to taste

In a wide skillet over medium heat, add two tablespoons of olive oil. Crumble the Italian sausage into the oil, stir frequently to brown, for about 5 minutes. Remove browned meat to a paper towel covered plate.

Add peppers and onion to the oil, sauté until broken down and onions are translucent – another five minutes. Stir in the minced garlic and sauté until fragrant – another minute. Pour the oregano over the mixture and stir in for about 30 seconds to release the flavor, then add the tomatoes and mix well. Return the meat to the skillet, reduce to a simmer, and cover. Simmer for 20 minutes or so to allow flavors to meld and serve over cheese grits.

10

THE RECIPE NOT WRITTEN DOWN

In high school, I worked at a grocery store after school. I worked from 4 to closing (which was 8 PM) during the week, and usually a good eight hours on Saturday, and would sometimes work on Sundays from 1 when we opened after the church was out, until 6 when we closed. Sunday was the worst because on Sundays you had to both open AND close.

It was a small town and a small grocery store. I didn't work every night, but most of them. I generally pulled 25 hours a week or more – probably more than was wise for a kid my age, but I loved it.

But the best part was after I got home. By the time we closed the store, it might be 9 before I got home during the week. Supper would be long over, and my brothers in bed, but Mom would leave dinner out for me, and I would fix myself a plate and heat it up in the microwave. Often she would then put everything away and go lay down and read, and Dad would sit up to watch the news before bed.

On this particular night, I had gotten in later than normal and was starving. Mom had fixed taco salad for supper, which was what she called it when she would spread crumbled tortilla chips on a plate, then cover the plate with iceberg lettuce and tomatoes and shredded cheese, which was then topped with "taco meat", which is what we called ground beef with an Old El Paso seasoning packet added, and jarred salsa and sour cream. It was very filling and good and seemed exotic in Marshall County, Mississippi in 1986.

All the ingredients were left out on the counter, waiting on me to put them together. Mom was already in bed, reading, and Dad was watching the end of a show, in anticipation of the news. I piled all the assorted goodness on my plate and, as I often did on those nights, sat in the living room with Dad and ate while we watched TV together.

When the show ended, I got up to put the food away. Dad followed me into the kitchen.

"Wait a minute", he said. "I need a snack."

He took down a large supper plate – one of the white Corelle plates with the blue flowers they had gotten as newlyweds – and spread chips over it in a single layer, edges just barely touching. Then he picked up the block of good sharp hoop cheese we always seemed to have in our refrigerator and, holding the box grater in his left hand, grated cheese over the tops of the chips in a dense layer, covering the chips until only the undulations of the chips under the cheese betrayed their existence.

He took this mounded plate of yellow marvelousness and put it in the microwave for 30 seconds, during which time the cheese melted and spread over the chips, flowing into the cracks and bubbling on top. He took it out, pulled a chip from the edge of the plate, watched

the melted cheese string stretch an improbable length before break-
ing, then picked it high in the air and, head tilted back, put the
whole thing in his mouth, cheese string first, the way some people
eat spaghetti.

Then he shut the microwave door and went into the living room
to watch the news. I had watched all this with curiosity, just waiting
to see where this was going. Suddenly, the spell broke.

"Wait, " I said. "I want some!"

"Well, make you some of your own. What do you want me to do,
write the recipe down for you?"

So I made some, exactly the same way, and just as I walked into
the living room, the news came on the TV. We sat together on the
couch, in silence, with nothing heard above the sound of the TV but
the crunching of chips and occasional sighs of satisfaction.

11

THE SICK DAY

It is said that smell is the oldest of the five senses we humans have. You need not convince me - I am sure of it. There have been times I've not smelled a thing in 30 years, and then I do, and I'm instantly taken back in time. It's as if the smell is somehow a shortcut to the exact spot in my brain where that memory hides.

I will never forget that hot summer night on Paris Island when I smelled rotting fruit. The smell of strawberries instantly transports me into a walk-in cooler in the backroom of the Big Star grocery in Byhalia, MS, where 16-year-old me would hide when I should have been working and eat the Louisiana strawberries that I should have been putting on the store shelves. I will always think of my great aunt's bathroom when I smell rusting metal.

And the smell of hot tuna always transports me back to my momma's kitchen on a day in 1980: A day I should have been in school but was home sick instead.

It was a cold day, and I had been running a fever all night. So mom let me lay on the couch and watch The Price is Right on TV instead of going to school.

I had dozed off somewhere before the Showcase Showdown, and she gently woke me. The TV was off, and I felt a bit better, and she sat on the couch beside me and asked if I was hungry.

"I'm about to fix some creamed tuna over toast," she said.

I told her I didn't know what that was.

"I know. But I love it, and your dad doesn't - he calls it cat food - and since it's just us today, I thought I would make some."

We walked into our tiny kitchen, and I drug a chair over to the stove to watch.

She got out a small pan and drained a can of tuna. We only had the kind packed in water because Dad was watching his cholesterol. She heated up a can of cream of mushroom soup, stirred in a can's worth of water, and added the tuna to it while it heated.

In the meantime, she put four slices of bread in our toaster, and when the toast was done, she tore it into small pieces, which she placed in the white Corelle bowls with the small blue flower trim they had gotten as newlyweds. Then, finally, she set them on the oak table my grandfather had rescued when the house caught fire in the 1930s.

She took a serving spoon from the drawer, spooned the tuna mixture over both our bowls, and then stirred it well to coat the hunks of bread with the ersatz roux.

To dad's point, the kitchen smelled vaguely of cat food, but not obnoxiously. At that moment, it just smelled good and safe.

Forty years later, I still love it - creamed tuna over toast, even if I don't make it that way anymore. In time, I would learn about bechamel sauce and seasoning and the value of aromatics. But that would all come later.

Mom and I didn't have a lot of things that were just ours - we still don't, actually - but our love of creamed tuna over toast was one of them. And to this day, when I don't feel particularly well, I will make a version of this dish and just know everything will be OK.

I want to go on record that there's nothing wrong with making it the way Mom did. If you are sick, have been pulling lots of shifts, or just don't have a lot of energy, spending 10 minutes dumping two cans into a pot and then pouring it over toasted bread may be all you have the energy for. And if that's true, then go for it.

But, if you find yourself with 15 minutes and a smidgen more energy, you can make something remarkable. These days, I often make this using chicken because my wife shares my dad's feelings about seafood, and I want to keep living here. But you can replace the chicken in this recipe with tuna and it still works.

Everything you will need for this is in your pantry, or at least it should be. Bread. Flour. Butter. Some leftover chicken. Salt. Pepper. Chicken broth, An onion. Milk. Love.

Before you get started, let's talk about chicken. You can use leftover chicken of any sort. White meat. Dark meat. Canned chicken. Leftover rotisserie chicken. Chicken legs you bought on clearance and poached specifically for this dish. It doesn't matter. Really. They all have different flavor profiles, but they are all good. You will need to shred it up, and you need about two cups of it. Or less if you are trying to stretch things.

You want to start with two tablespoons of butter, which you put in a medium-sized saucepan over medium heat.

While it's melting, take a small onion, and dice it fine. You don't need a lot of onion, and if I'm feeling fancy and it's after payday, I would probably use a large shallot for this, and if it's a few days before payday, I would probably use the 1/2 an onion sitting in the crisper drawer in a ziplock bag leftover from God knows what.

Sweat the onions for about five minutes in the melted butter. You don't want to let them burn, so you may have to reduce the heat. Then put in two tablespoons of flour, and, using your whisk, get the flour coated in the melted butter. Just like when you are making milk gravy, you don't want the flour to burn. This is a white sauce, so all you want is the flour and oil to be mixed well.

Slowly add a cup of half and half, a 1/4 cup or so at a time, whisking all the while, until it's all mixed in. Then do the same with the chicken broth - add it slowly, while whisking, until it is a lovely velvety smooth, and probably slightly yellow. That color is one of my favorite colors. The smell right now is something else, too.

If you are feeling fancy, this is where you throw in about half a cup of what my people call English peas, and you probably call green peas or sweet peas. Little green round peas, fresh if you have them but most likely frozen, is what we're going for here. And then add the chicken, stirring it all in, so the lovely creamy sauce covers the chicken and peas, and the peas look like little green islands in a light yellow sea.

You want this to simmer for about 5-10 minutes to both warm up the peas and chicken, and to thicken the sauce. If it gets too thick, you can drizzle in a bit of hot water while stirring and also remember that it will thicken a bit as it sits and cools.

While the sauce is simmering, start making toast - two to three slices per person is about right. When the toast is done, I like to rip it into rough chunks about 2 inches square. Then pour a generous half cup of sauce over the top, and if you have any, sprinkle the top with fresh chopped parsley to be fancy. Honestly, if I make this when I feel bad, I have been known to eat it out of a bowl while leaning against the kitchen counter.

This is one of my favorite meals. In sociology, there is a concept called "code switching". It describes the phenomenon where you speak differently to different audiences. How I speak to my best friend is different than how I speak to my grandmother, which is different than how I speak at a job interview.

Historically, it also describes how people from one class move between groups - the formal register you use at the job interview is different than how you talk at home. Code switching lets you move back and forth, fitting in in various groups. This recipe code switches well.

For brunch, you can serve this precisely as it is written, but over busted open biscuits, the way you would do sausage gravy. If company comes over, I will serve this over rice, with parsley sprinkled on top for some color. You can use tuna like my momma did in exchange for the chicken if you have pescatarians over for dinner. However, we didn't know any pescatarians and would have been convinced they were a cult had we heard the word. You can also use ground beef if you want something a bit heavier, which, minus the peas, is how they served this to us in the Marines.

This will serve two hungry people or 4 polite ones, but it scales up perfectly - 2 tablespoons of fat and flour and a cup of broth for every cup of dairy.

I should also say that you are not confined to using half and half here. Go buck wild and use whipping cream if you are a generally optimistic person, but honestly, whole milk is what I use most often because that's what's in the fridge when I get the urge to make this. Some of you are scared of your food and will be tempted to use skim milk. While I discourage this, I can't stop you.

Some people, I have learned, just want to watch the world burn.

Creamed chicken over toast

Ingredients

- 1-2 cups of shredded cooked chicken

- 2 Tablespoons of butter

- 2 Tablespoons of all-purpose flour

- ½ cup of diced onion

- 1 cup of whole milk

- 1 cup of chicken broth

- ½ cup of frozen green peas

- 4 pieces of toast, roughly torn (not cut) into 2-inch squares.

Melt the butter in a medium saucepan over medium heat. Sweat the diced onion in the melted butter for 5 minutes or so until they are soft and translucent (you may need to reduce the heat to keep from burning the onions). Next, add the flour to the onions, whisking as you do so the onions get coated in the flour. When it's all in and incorporated with the butter and onions, slowly add the half and half a quarter of a cup or so at a time, all the while whisking. Then, do the same with the chicken broth. Add the green peas and chicken, stir well, and allow to simmer for 5-10 minutes to thicken. Serve over the toast squares.

12

MY FAVORITE SANDWICH

Until my late teens, my Dad worked for a propane company.

Like Hank Hill, my father sold propane and propane accessories.

In rural Mississippi, propane is a big deal. I live in town now, and we have natural gas piped in, but folks who live out in the county buy propane, and a giant truck comes out to your house and fills up a huge tank, and that is what fuels your water heater and your cookstove and your heater. Every small town in Mississippi has at least one propane dealer, and in my hometown for most of my childhood, that dealership was run by my daddy.

Now, they sold propane, but the propane accessories was where the money was. The showroom at the front of his building had propane cook stoves, propane fish cookers, and propane grills for sale. The markup on these was high, and after all, the more things you owned that used propane, the more propane you would buy. So every summer, they would have an Open House of sorts, where they would do some sort of sale and set up a grill in the parking lot in front of the building, and there might be balloons and, to highlight the cooking ability of this grill, Dad would put a couple of pounds of bologna on the rotisserie.

It was smart on a number of levels: Bologna was cheap, so this promotion was low cost. It highlighted a rotisserie accessory, which most folks didn't have, and so they couldn't replicate it without buying one. It smelled amazing, so it intrigued people who stopped by. And it just tasted good.

It wasn't complicated: He went to the meat counter in the Big Star grocery and bought a 5-pound chub of bologna, which is just bologna that hasn't been sliced. It looks like a huge hot dog more than anything else. It has a red plastic skin, which must be peeled away. Then it was threaded onto the rotisserie spit and scored about a quarter inch deep along its length in a criss-cross pattern. Then it was cooked for a good hour or two over medium heat and was periodically basted with a cheap bottled barbeque sauce.

The heat made the surface split along the score marks, and the sauce would seep into the cracks, and the barbeque sauce would sort of candy on the surface. He would keep one going all day, and would have another cut up into small chunks, which were speared on toothpicks for the customers to try as samples. But one advantage of having a dad who was the manager was that you didn't just get the small samples: You got a barbeque bologna sandwich.

It involved a hamburger bun, toasted. On it, you put a dollop of cheap bottled sauce, a half-inch thick slice of barbeque bologna, all topped by a generous scoop of cole slaw. It won't taste right unless it is served on a cheap paper plate, accompanied by a handful of Golden Flake potato chips, and paired with an ice cold Coke in a glass bottle that was purchased for a quarter from the cold drink box in the warehouse.

And for best results, it should be handed to you by someone who loves you.

13

WHAT THEY EAT IN HEAVEN

No dish ever got my mom as upset as steak and gravy. As I have relayed elsewhere in these pages, there was an elderly couple that lived next door to us on three acres my grandmother had sold them when our money got tight.

Doc was a retired truck farmer and well digger, and she was a farmer's wife who cooked every day of her life. In her simple farmhouse kitchen, I learned the power of simple ingredients, done with care and love, to transform themselves into something spectacular.

Aunt Monty's food was legendary. Her beef stew was unduplicatable. Her plum roll was a simple treat with which we marked the holidays, and her biscuits were a daily treat. She and I would pick wild plums and muscadines every summer and put up countless pints of jelly.

But her steak and gravy caused fights in our house. We Hollowell children seldom ate beef - it was expensive. Except for the ground beef that went into meatloaf or spaghetti, it was virtually unknown in our household. So, when Monty would make steak and gravy, it was a rare, exotic treat for us. One we talked about to no end.

"We had steak and gravy at Monty's house," we said. "It was soooo good."

"Monty's steak and gravy is the best food in the whole world," I told my mom, who was just trying to survive over here, working to put enough calories on the table to keep us alive.

My mom was a competent cook but did not enjoy it, and meals in our house tended to prioritize ease and economy. That she was 28 years old and constantly compared to a 70-year-old cook legendary in our community probably did nothing to help the situation.

For my birthday one year, mom made me steak and gravy as a treat. She called Monty to get the scoop. The way Mom tells the story, the conversation wasn't exactly enlightening. Monty had been fixing this for her whole life. She added enough salt, a handful of flour, a knob of butter, and so on. She pounded the steak until it was "thin enough" and would use a small onion and put the whole thing in a "slow" oven. To someone who learned to cook from the Betty Crocker cookbook, it was exasperating.

But Momma tried. Lord, did Momma try.

The kitchen was covered in flour. The house was filled with loud sounds - WHACK, WHACK, WHACK, as she pounded the steak with a tenderizer hammer. Grease splattered on the stovetop as the steaks sizzled in the skillet. A box of potato flakes we had gotten at the county office when we got our commodities box made an appearance.

It was ... good. In fact, had I not been trying to compare it to Monty's, it would have been one of the best meals of my childhood. I was too young to know that some meals belong to a particular time and place and are unduplicatable elsewhere. That when we try to make those dishes, it is not to get the exact taste but to bring back all the memories attached to the food itself - much the way the postcard in the photo album is a pale imitation of the seashore but serves to remind us of the reality and existence of it.

But I didn't know any of that yet. So instead, when asked, I told the truth: It's good but not as good as Monty's. Eight-year-olds have a brutal, unkind honesty about them. Mom walked out of the room. It was probably for the best.

These days, things are different. I make decent money, and beef no longer needs to be a rare delicacy, but I seldom eat it, as I never really gained a desire for it. While other people want a big steak to celebrate, I would rather have a bowl of beans and cornbread or a big plate heaping with jambalaya or red beans and rice. But if I were on death row and offered any meal I could choose as my last request, it would be steak, gravy, and mashed potatoes.

It goes together simply enough, being the sort of dish that takes time but not much effort. Having given up all hope of duplicating Monty's process, I cheat.

Monty always bought round steak if it was on sale, or sometimes she would get a chuck roast she cut into thin steaks. The cut really doesn't matter - you are going to cook the hound out of it, anyway.

But what I do, more often than not, is buy what the supermarket calls "minute steaks" or "cubed steak", which is just a lean piece of beef that they ran through the tenderizer machine, leaving it covered in dimples. It is custom made for steak and gravy.

Also, Monty would have used russet potatoes - white potatoes, she would have called them - but I tend to use Yukon Golds, which taste buttery to me and mash well. But I think Monty would forgive the improvisations on her technique. It's still good, even though it will never taste as good as Monty's did. Sometimes, if I'm honest, I wonder if Monty's tasted as good as Monty's did.

The last time I made steak and gravy, it went like this:

You should know up front that this will take about 3 hours to do right. Of course, you can do it in less time, but it won't be as tender, and if done slowly, you can cut this with a spoon.

I got out the deep skillet and put four tablespoons of shortening in it to melt and turned the oven on to 350 to preheat.

While waiting, I put half a cup of flour in a shallow bowl and added a teaspoon of black pepper, a teaspoon of salt, and a half teaspoon each of garlic powder and cayenne pepper. I stirred it well.

After dredging the cubed steaks through the flour mixture, I put them in the skillet to brown—about two minutes a side until the flour had formed a crisp crust, but the interiors were still not finished. I did them in batches, putting them on a cooling rack as they finished.

Now you need to make gravy. This is brown milk gravy, which is different than the brown water gravy you might use for something like Salisbury steaks.

In the melted shortening still in the pan's bottom, I sauteed a handful (maybe a quarter cup?) of diced onion until brown, then added a few tablespoons of the flour dredge that was left over.

If you have made white milk gravy (what they call a bechamel sauce in fancy places), this is different from that. In milk gravy, you do not want the flour to be brown. In this version, you want it to brown but not burn. It takes some stirring for a few minutes, but you are going for a color around that of a paper grocery bag or perhaps a shade darker. You do not want it to be the color of coffee.

After it was all browned, I added enough water to make a thin gravy, into which I slid the breaded steaks. If you then decide it wasn't quite dark enough, you can add a couple of teaspoons of Worcestershire sauce and stir well before you add the steaks.

I then put a lid on the skillet and slid it into the oven, where it sat and bubbled away for about two hours.

While it cooks, the gravy will thicken up a good deal. This is why you want your gravy thin at the beginning - it cooks down in the oven. Remove the steaks with a pancake turner - they will be tender and may try to fall apart on you if you are not careful - and put them on a plate. I then add a bit of half and half to thin the gravy back down, whisking furiously as I add it until the gravy thins out. I then slide the steaks back in, put the lid on, and then put it over a low burner while I prepare the mashed potatoes.

Mashed potatoes were a rarity for us until the government began handing out commodity boxes at the county office. Potatoes don't keep well in our hot, humid environment, so we bought them in 5-pound bags from the grocery store. But in late spring, the potatoes would come in from the garden, and they would reappear on our plates.

But perhaps I should explain the commodity boxes. The USDA began handing out surplus food to people deemed to be "in need," which was pretty much my whole county. So, you went to the county office and stood in line, and you would get a box of non-perishable food, like rice, corn flakes, potato flakes, and the holy grail, American cheese. It was the best cheese - it melted well and made the best grilled cheese sandwiches you have ever had.

But the point is, most of the mashed potatoes I ate as a child came out of a box unless Monty made them.

Mashed potatoes get a bad rap as something labor-intensive, but they really aren't. You simply peel four potatoes about the size of your fist, and if you are in a hurry, quarter them. This will help them cook faster. Put them in a saucepan, cover them with water and heat to a boil.

While you're waiting for the water to boil, add a couple of teaspoons of salt and three smashed garlic cloves. Now, you can omit the garlic or double it - this depends on your disposition and what sort of house you were raised in. We are garlic people. But we recognize some folks aren't. Live and let live, I say. After all, you can't help it if people don't know what's good.

After 12 minutes, start checking your potatoes. You want the point of a knife to slide into the potato easily, but you don't want it to crumble. Pour off the water but leave the potatoes in the pan. Some folks remove the garlic at this point, but I do not. I just mash it in with the potatoes.

For the next part, you need a potato masher. The best kind has a wiggly pattern, made of heavy wire, that you will curse often as it gets hung up in that drawer you keep all your utensils in. They make the kind that are round, but avoid these, as they just cause problems. These are mashed potatoes we are making here; they are not, Lord help you, whipped potatoes. You cannot do this with any device that plugs into a wall or has a battery - you need a masher.

Right there in the pan that you cooked them in, add a half a stick of butter and a quarter cup of half and half or, if you have a guilty conscience, 2% milk. The point is, it will all work here, but the half and half tastes better.

Now commence to mashing.

There's no secret to it: you just keep mashing until you get the consistency you want. I sort of start at the edges of the pan and mash toward the center, going around the edge, turning the pan as I go. If the mixture seems too thick, add a splash of half and half as you mash. But do it with an easy hand, as it's easy to thin it down too much, and then you are just stuck with thin potatoes.

If you are taking these some place fancy, you can put them in a casserole dish, smooth them out like you are icing a cake, and then sprinkle paprika on top for color. But mostly we just put them on a plate straight from the pan, with a dollop of butter on top, then cover them with the gravy from the steak.

When served with a portion of the steak and a serving of canned English peas (which, if you are 7 years old you stir into the potatoes), this is the epitome of wonderful from my childhood, and what I am to this day firmly convinced they serve for supper every night in heaven.

Steak and gravy

Ingredients
Preheat the oven to 350 degrees.

- 4 tablespoons of shortening

- 1/2 cup of flour

- 1 tsp black pepper

- 1 tsp salt

- 1/2 tsp garlic powder

- 1/2 tsp cayenne pepper

- 4 cubed steaks

- 1/4 cup diced onion

- hot water - perhaps 2 cups

- 2 teaspoons of Worcestershire sauce

- half and half

Mix the flour, pepper, garlic powder, salt, and cayenne pepper in a wide bowl or a deep plate.

To a heavy skillet (one that has an oven-safe lid) over medium heat, add the shortening and let it melt.

Dredge the cube steaks through the flour mixture, pushing them deep into the mixture on both sides of the steak. Place them into the melted grease to brown - about 2-3 minutes per side, allowing the flour to crust. You will probably have to do these in batches, and a wire cooling rack is the best place for them when they are finished.

To make the gravy, sauté the onion in the residual grease until it is tender, then add about four tablespoons of the leftover flour dredge. If you don't have 4 tablespoons of flour left, add what you have.

Use a wire whisk to stir the mixture frequently until it turns the color of a paper bag. Then, while whisking, slowly add the hot water until the flour mixture becomes a thin gravy. It will thicken as it cooks, so you want to err on the thin side. Add Worcestershire sauce, stir well with the whisk, and then slide the steaks into the gravy.

Cook for two hours. Remove the steaks, thin gravy if needed by adding half and half a tablespoon at a time while whisking furiously. Return steaks to skillet and put over a low burner to stay warm until served.

14

LOST RECIPES

He was my dad's half-brother from my grandmother's first marriage and was 23 years older than Dad. After her first husband's death, my grandmother refused to remarry until her son was out of the house, as she thought it would be unfair to him. Her chief concern was that a new husband would treat his stepson differently from his natural children. She had grown up with a wicked stepmother herself and knew the risks.

My uncle was a good man, tall and handsome, with shocking red hair and long, deft fingers. He was solidly middle-class, having worked as a union meat cutter until he opened a barbecue restaurant. His wife was a short woman with improbable blond hair that was always tortured into shape and held against its will by a generous application of some sort of shellac. Their grown daughter had married a musician, and while they all said the word "musician," you got the sense from how it was said they meant it to say degenerate or ne'er-do-well.

Their house was a large brick colonial on a cul-de-sac, with a yard meant for looking at and not playing in. There was a room designated as the parlor, which children could not be in and in which no one ever laughed. My uncle's wife was a woman to whom propriety mattered and firmly believed children should be seen and not heard, and if she had it her way, only seen from a distance.

They had a dining room that one got the sense nobody ate at the rest of the year, and it had a massive table with place settings and food set out in bowls and trays, served family style. People who hadn't prayed out loud in 364 days would ask the Lord's blessing over the food. We ate food that had attachments and memories, like Aunt Louise's cranberry sauce and Mom's fudge pies.

The cranberry sauce was nothing special, except it was unlike anything I had ever seen. Mom always bought the canned cranberry sauce that held its shape when you put it on a serving dish, which you sliced like a stick of bologna and served.

But Aunt Louise's cranberry sauce was magical - it was both tart and sweet, defying all known laws of science, and was more like a thick jelly or lumpy syrup. It was a magical concoction you could put on anything served at the Thanksgiving feast. Chicken and dressing? Sure. Turkey? Of course! Mashed potatoes? Why not. Butter beans? It's worth a shot. And leftover chicken and dressing sandwiches? It was practically required.

The cranberry sauce was served in a low casserole dish used for no other purpose the rest of the year. It always had a garnish of semi-circular slices of orange, peel intact, standing around the edges, much like the way you do the edges of a pan with vanilla wafers if you are making banana pudding.

Louise was my grandmother's sister, and when Louise left her husband because of his drunkenness and my grandmother's first husband died unexpectedly, they moved in together. Louise helped raise my uncle through the Great Depression and World War II, working the night shift while my grandmother worked the day. And my uncle loved Louise's cranberry sauce. I do not know the origins of the cranberry sauce she made, nor do I have the canonical recipe handed down on a dirty index card from the sacred recipe box. Louise's three cookbooks that were in her house are now in mine, and it isn't in any of them, either.

One would imagine that fresh cranberries, which can only be grown in Northern climes, were scarce in Dyersburg, TN in the 1930s when she was learning how to be a housewife, but somewhere along the line, she picked it up, even if she never passed it down.

The way I do it now is an amalgamation of memory and practicality and experimentation. You are going to need a quarter-cup of orange juice. If you are not the sort of person who routinely has orange juice in your house, you might want to just buy a bag of oranges and juice a few of them for this, as you will need an orange for the zest and another for the garnish. But you can also just buy a small container of orange juice and two oranges, and nobody will know the difference.

Put the orange juice in a saucepan over low heat, add 1/2 a cup of sugar and 3/4 a cup of water and stir it well. As it heats up, you need to zest an orange. I know I just lost some of y'all, and others have put down this book and are now Googling "How to zest an orange." It's not hard - stick with me.

You need a fine grater to do this right. If you have a box grater, it's the side that looks like a bunch of tiny bumps. (You may also have a zester, but if you do, you probably don't need me to tell you how to use it.) Just hold the grater in your left hand and the orange in your right and you rub the orange on the grater, making orange peel dust. You only want the actual orange part, not the bitter white pith that is underneath it.

If you don't have a box grater, you can do a passable imitation by using a vegetable peeler and peeling the orange with it, again avoiding the pith, and then dicing the peel into a very fine dice. However you do it, you want the zest of the whole orange. The orange itself should be mostly white when you are done with it. Add the zest to the saucepan and turn the heat up to medium and stir it occasionally until the sugar has completely dissolved.

In my part of the world, around the holidays, you can buy fresh cranberries at the grocery store in the produce department in clear plastic bags that weigh about 12 ounces. Rinse them in a colander and then add the fresh cranberries to the saucepan, stir it well to coat them with the mixture, and then crank up the heat until it boils, then turn it down until it's a low simmer. Let it simmer for 20 minutes until the sauce has thickened some. (It will thicken more as it cools, so don't fret too much about this).

It's done at this point, but if you are a presentation person, you can do as we do and slice your remaining orange in half along its equator and then into 1/8th inch thick slices, which you line up in an overlapping scalloped edge along the perimeter of a round serving dish. Then pour the cranberry sauce in the middle, allowing it to press the oranges to the edge of the dish. This is a colorful dish, with wine-red cranberry sauce and bright orange slices. This is an excellent opportunity to add a colorful serving dish to the mix.

I said we always brought my mom's fudge pies to my uncle's house, but that isn't technically true: They were Ms. Dunning's pies. At least, they were originally.

It all started with a spiral-bound church cookbook that the Methodist church of my childhood put out in the late 70s as a fundraiser. It's blue, with a drawing of the church on the front—the church as I remember it before the fellowship hall, the new sanctuary was built, and they bought the electric sign that has the time, temperature, and the announcement about the upcoming revival that sits out front.

The cookbook has spots and stains, more on some pages than others, so you can track our preferences and dislikes, with each spotted page a vote for the dishes on that page. It suffers from specificity of categories, having a chapter labeled Pies, another Cakes, another Cookies and Candies, and then yet another called Desserts, as a catch-all just in case some sweet delicacy slipped through uncatalogued.

After this cookbook showed up, we started having chocolate fudge pies at every holiday gathering and potluck dinner. Wherever 3 or more were gathered, there was a fudge pie. Birthdays? Fudge pies. Christmas? Fudge pies. Thanksgiving?

Fudge pies, my friend. It was fudge pies all the way down.

The recipe in my copy of the cookbook has been so altered, with additions and subtractions and alterations made over the ensuing 40 years in various inks that it's not really fair to call it Ms. Dunning's recipe anymore.

For example, the original recipe is for two pies—that's what it says, anyway. But remember, this book was published in 1978, and the recipe was old then. It was made for 8-inch pie crusts, and they don't sell those pre-made anymore. I recently tried to buy some 8-inch pie pans and had a devil of a time trying to find any. It seems our pies are all super-sized now, with nine or 9.5-inch pans being all there is. So, over the years, we have changed this somewhat to work with one 9-inch pre-made frozen pie crust.

Let's talk about pie crust for a second here. You can make your crust from scratch, or you can use one of those frozen ones from the store, or you can buy one that you roll out yourself from the cold box at the store by the whop-em biscuits. I won't blame you, whatever you do, having done all the above at various times.

However, know that the frozen ones are often "deep dish" pie crusts, and this won't fill one of those up, but will still make a tasty, albeit thin, pie, nonetheless.

There's no shame in a pre-made crust. However, pastry is a whole distinct skill set from cooking, and most of us don't make enough pies to learn how to do it well. I'm going to assume you bought a 9-inch regular frozen pie crust, mainly because if you are the sort of person who enjoys making their own crust, you probably don't need my help with it.

To start, set your frozen crust out to thaw. It won't take long—it will probably thaw during the 10 minutes you take to mix this up - and preheat your oven to 350 degrees.

Mix a cup and a half of sugar and three tablespoons of cocoa powder in a mixing bowl until they are well blended. I recommend sifting the cocoa with a flour sifter. If you don't have a flour sifter, you can put it in a sieve and tap it until all the cocoa comes out the bottom. If you don't have a sieve, you can just dump it in and take your chances and probably be OK, but I still always sift mine.

Then, add half a stick of melted butter and stir it all until it is well mixed. I'm not even going to lie—most often, this was margarine growing up, but it's butter now. When you know better, you do better.

Add 2 eggs, a teaspoon of vanilla (don't cheap out here - always use the real stuff when dealing with cocoa), a pinch of salt, a 1/4 cup of flour, and a half cup of evaporated milk, and stir until well blended. Don't go out and buy a mixer for this—just a whisk or wooden spoon will do fine. It's pretty forgiving—my sister-in-law once forgot the salt and added it after it was in the pan, and it still worked out.

The mixture is thin—you will be sure you screwed it up. Nope, it just looks thin. Put your pie pan on a cookie sheet and then pour the mixture into the pie pan. The reason for putting it on the cookie sheet is that it's easier to pick up a cookie sheet than a pie pan.

Slide the cookie sheet into the preheated oven on the bottom shelf and set the timer for 35 minutes. It won't be ready in 35 minutes, but it will be getting close. It will probably take closer to 45 or 50, but it has snuck up on me before and been burned as a result. You will know it's done when it's firm in the middle—at 35 minutes, the center will probably still jiggle when you shake the pan.

Another reason for checking on it around 35 or 40 minutes is to make sure the crust doesn't burn. I take a sheet of aluminum foil bigger than the pie and crease it corner to corner and then lay it on top of the pie around the 40-minute mark to keep the crust from burning. Creasing it keeps it off the top of the pie filling—you don't want the foil to touch the surface of the pie or else it makes an unholy mess. Of course, it will still taste good, but you would not dare bring it to the potluck for fear of the talk that would follow you.

Now, some warnings: The surface of this pie might crack. That is not a defect. I have had days when it took almost an hour of checking to get this pie done. I can't explain why, as I do it exactly the same way every time. The ways of both the Lord and fudge pies are mysterious. Check every five minutes after 35 minutes and see if the center is still jiggly. When it stops jiggling, it's done. It will firm up a bit when it's cool, but not enough to take a chance on a jiggly pie from the oven.

Growing up, we often put Cool Whip on this, but then again, we all did things when we were young that we are ashamed of later. These days, I like homemade whipped cream, or, on the third day after Thanksgiving, I will often eat it straight from the pie pan while leaning against the counter.

After the desserts were consumed, my uncle and the musician would watch football, and Dad would sit there with them to be polite, but he had no interest in the game. I would play with the other children upstairs, out of the way. The women all talked in the kitchen and tried to put order to things before we would pack up and head back to the country, to our small rectangular home on 33 acres, where the cups did not match, there were no rooms that were not used and there were whole fields where one could run and romp.

Fudge pie

Ingredients

- 1 1/2 cup sugar

- 3 tablespoons of cocoa powder

- 1/2 stick butter, melted

- 2 eggs, beaten

- 1/2 cup evaporated milk

- 1 teaspoon vanilla

- 1/4 cup flour

- pinch of salt

- 9-inch unbaked pie crust

Preheat the oven to 350 degrees.

Sift the cocoa into the sugar to avoid clumping. Stir in the melted butter until well blended, then add the rest of the ingredients while stirring. (Add the flour slowly while stirring to avoid clumps.) Pour the mixture into an unbaked 9-inch regular (not deep dish) pie crust and cook for 35-50 minutes (see note) until firm in the middle.

Cranberry sauce

Ingredients

- 1/4 cup orange juice, freshly squeezed if you have it

- The zest of one orange

- Another orange

- 1/2 cup sugar

- 1 (12-ounce) bag fresh cranberries

In a medium saucepan, combine orange juice, orange zest, sugar and 3/4 of a cup of water over medium heat. Cook, stirring the mixture occasionally, until the sugar has dissolved.

Stir in the cranberries and boil them. Reduce the heat and let it simmer until the sauce has thickened, about 15 minutes. Slice the remaining orange into semicircles and garnish the serving bowl with them before pouring in the cranberry sauce. Let it cool completely before serving.

15

THE BEST IN THE WORLD

A while back, I was interviewed for a podcast, and we talked about food and how it figures into our memories. And I had a throwaway line in there where I was talking about the power of food, and I said that the best meal you ever had and your favorite meal were probably two different meals.

My point was that the feelings we associate with food are often separate from the actual quality of the food. This is why my favorite way to eat hot dogs has nothing to do with the best-tasting hot dog I ever had.

No matter when you are reading this, the best-tasting hot dog I ever had was about two weeks ago, in my kitchen. It was the Kirkland bun-length all-beef hotdog, from Costco. It was on a Nature's Own butter roll, and it was outfitted with dill pickle relish and Dijon mustard.

They are in our rotation, and maybe once a month when we need supper in a hurry, I will steam some hot dogs and bake some tater tots and have supper on the table in 20 minutes, with very little mess to clean up.

It's an amazing hot dog. Really. But it's not my favorite.

I was six years old and was staying at Monty and Doc's house. They were retired farmers who lived next door to us and served as my surrogate grandparents because all of mine were dead or far away.

Monty was the best cook in the world—I know I said so dozens of times, and usually to my mom when she tried to replicate something I had eaten cooked by Monty, and Mom's version was found wanting.

"Of course, it's not as good as Monty's, Mom. Monty's the best cook in the world."

This was probably not, in retrospect, the most empowering thing my mom ever heard.

But anyway, I'm staying at Monty and Doc's. And for lunch that day, she told me we were having hot dogs.

I loved hot dogs. Mostly, Mom just boiled them, and we put them on buns with mustard and ketchup (don't judge—I was young and foolish). When times were tight, we would use white bread instead of buns. Sometimes when we went camping, we would eat them grilled. But I had never had Monty's hot dogs—I just knew these were going to be great!

I knew something was up when she got out a cast-iron skillet. She then sliced the dogs—the bright red linked dogs you bought at the butcher counter, not the "regular" hot dogs Mom always bought—from end to end. Then she put a dab of bacon grease in the middle of the skillet and turned the stove on medium, and I watched the fat melt and coat the bottom of the skillet. She picked up the skillet and turned it first this way and then that, coating the bottom of the skillet with a thin sheen of fat.

She put the sliced dogs, cut side up, in the skillet and cooked them until they got a slight crust on the outside, then flipped them over. They would often be curled from the heat, and she would take her turner and press the cut side down against the bottom of the skillet until it, too, was crusted.

While they were cooking, she had put white bread (light bread, we called it then) under the broiler to toast. Then, she slathered one piece with yellow mustard, put one and a half hot dogs (three strips) on top of that, and then coated the other piece of toast with mayonnaise, and the sandwich was made.

I protested. "I don't like mayonnaise on my hot dogs," I told her.

"Have you ever had a hot dog sandwich before?" she asked.

Well, no, I admitted.

She told me that meant I didn't know if I liked it or not, and to sit down and eat my sandwich.

So, I did. And that was the day I learned I love mayonnaise on a hot dog sandwich.

16

THE WORST REASON TO DO ANYTHING

She lived alone on 40 acres, 10 miles from a town of 800 people, in a drafty old farmhouse. While she owned a car, she could not drive. It never occurred to me at the time, but Aunt Louise, my grandmother's sister, was intensely lonely out there.

Lonnie was her second husband, and he had owned land out in rural Mississippi, so when they got married she moved from Memphis to his house. It had been his parents' house, actually. Lonnie had grown up in it and then had lived in it with his first wife, and when he moved Louise in, she insisted on major changes. The kitchen was moved to another room, the bathroom was upgraded, and she turned the old kitchen into a storage room.

I asked her one time why she moved the kitchen.

"There wasn't anything wrong, really, with the old kitchen. But it wasn't mine. It was hers", she said, meaning the first wife. "I told him if I was moving in there, he was going to make the house the way I like it. "

And he did. Aunt Louise took no crap.

She had lived in town all her life – in Dyersburg, and then in Memphis. And so moving to the middle of nowhere was a big deal for her. And when he had died in 1971, she was alone in that house, with her two dogs – Festus and Princess.

I only knew her when she was alone. We would go over on Saturday and take her grocery shopping in town, and occasionally we took her into Memphis to her doctor's appointment, and often I would spend the night there when Mom and Dad went out somewhere and would be home late. I loved staying at Aunt Louise's house.

I don't know if she even knew the word feminist, but when I learned of it, Aunt Louise spring to mind. She was so perfectly herself. Virtually every woman I knew was in some way defined by a man. Mom was married to Dad, and did things that benefited him. Monty was married to Mr. Doc, and cooked and did his laundry. But Aunt Louise just took care of herself. She was the most independent woman I knew growing up.

She wore pants, carried a pistol in her purse, drank whisky, smoked hand-rolled cigarettes, and would, when she got down, drunk dial her friends back in Memphis. She refused to take the Lord's supper in church, read Earle Stanly Gardener and Agatha Christie, watched Barnaby Jones and Perry Mason and Gunsmoke on TV, and cooked for herself and her dogs.

She constantly amazed and delighted me. Her death when I was 12 was devastating.

Sometimes she ate cereal for supper. I told her that everybody knew that cereal was for breakfast, and she told me she was a grown woman and could do whatever she wanted to, and that the worst reason to do anything was that everyone told you that you were supposed to do it that way.

She drank three cups of coffee every morning, but always made a full pot. The leftover coffee she mixed with evaporated milk and poured over a handful of crushed crackers and served that to her dogs. Yes, her dogs got coffee for breakfast each morning.

I never asked why the dogs got coffee – some things you are probably better not knowing.

Once, when I was staying over, Mom had dropped me off after supper, and so we were sitting at her table, watching Barnaby Jones while waiting to go to bed when she announced she was hungry. I told her I had already eaten, and she told me that she had too, but that a nice thing about living by yourself was that you could absolutely eat two suppers if you wanted to.

She got up and rummaged around in the pantry, and pulled out a can of Showboat Pork and Beans. She put them on the stove to warm, and then she pulled a package of hot dogs from the freezer and took two out. She sliced the frozen dogs directly into the beans and then covered them as they simmered.

After we had eaten, she got out a half-gallon of vanilla ice cream and a can of Hershey's syrup, and we gave a scoop of ice cream to the dogs, because of course we did, and we ate ice cream and watched Perry Mason and I told her I was always going to live alone, so I could stay up late and eat ice cream whenever I wanted.

"You don't have to live alone to stay up late and eat ice cream whenever you want", she told me.

"It's just easier if you do."

17

CELEBRATING EVERY DAY

When I was a boy, my best friend in the world was a boy my age named Paul. He lived a mile and a quarter away from me, and our families both went to the same church.

Paul was adopted, and his parents were around 50 when they adopted him as an infant, so Paul always had the "old" parents. My parents were 21 when I was born, so his parents were nearly 30 years older than mine. It always felt like going to another culture to be invited to their house.

His father was a tall man who worked in a warehouse. His thick, ropy muscled arms were tattooed, with a silhouette of a naked lady putting on her panties on one forearm and an anchor on the other—relics of his time in the Navy. At the time, I thought this was the coolest thing in the world. I remember asking him if the naked lady was Paul's mom, and he just giggled.

He also had an old Ford Falcon car that he had turned into a pickup truck with the help of a cutting torch and some plywood. If there was anything more fabulous than having a naked lady tattooed on your arm, it was making your own pickup truck. I thought Paul had the most incredible parents in the world.

His mom didn't work outside the home, so sometimes I would play at Paul's house when it met my mom's convenience for me not to be home. And sometimes, I would get invited to stay for supper.

Now, understand that in the world I grew up in, older people could cook fantastic food, and young people mostly could not. So, if you got invited to eat at Paul's house, what with his parents being older, the odds were definitely in your favor.

This leads us to the day my life changed forever—when his mom served chicken and dressing for supper.

Don't get me wrong, I've eaten chicken and dressing my whole life. We had it, or a variation of it, every Thanksgiving and Christmas for as long as I can remember. It was one of the things Aunt Louise made and brought when we went to my uncle's house for the holidays. When she died, Mom started making it, but used sausage rather than chicken because Dad wasn't a fan of poultry of any sort. In classic Dad joke fashion, he said it was because it was "fowl meat".

But we never ate it just because. Instead, it was a "holiday food," sort of the way people never fix green bean casserole on a weeknight. But that day, in that single-wide trailer just a half mile outside Possum Trot, Mississippi, I learned a life-changing truth: You can eat good food any time you want—you don't need a special reason.

Some celebration foods are long and involved to make, but dressing isn't one of them. If you plan ahead, it's easily the sort of thing you can make in an hour and a half, and most of that is cooking time. What's more, it uses up a lot of leftovers and is cheap as chips to make.

We might as well address the elephant in the room and define our terms. The divide between dressing and stuffing is mainly semantic and has a lot to do with geography and who your people are. The classic definition says that stuffing is put inside the bird, and dressing is cooked in a pan like a casserole. Still, the Stovetop people do neither and yet proudly proclaim that they are making stuffing.

Others say it is a matter of materials—dressing being cornbread and stuffing being wheat bread. And I have heard the North/South (or Black/White) divide argument as well. But in my experience, dressing is cooked in a pan, like a casserole. It is made primarily of cornbread. And it is moist, ideally cooked with meat in it, and served with gravy. In any event, I know nothing about stuffing, having come from dressing people.

You need some cornbread, ideally made without sugar. Don't come after me—this is not the place for Jiffy cornbread mix. It just won't taste right and is too moist, anyway. You want dry cornbread, so I make a double batch of my Southern Cornbread, which I have shared elsewhere in these pages, the day before and leave it out on the counter overnight so it will dry up.

You need a little bit of wheat bread. Traditionally, folks saved leftover biscuits for this, but since we don't bake them daily as the old folks did, I toast up three pieces of sandwich bread and call it a day. If you are more put-together than I am, you could save your bread heels for this dish.

As I said earlier, my Aunt Louise (as well as Paul's mom and most everyone I knew) used chicken in this, but my mom always used pork breakfast sausage. If you are using chicken, about two cups of shredded meat, ideally dark meat (I like thighs for this), is pretty much perfect. In a pinch, you could use a rotisserie chicken from the grocery store. If you are on the ball, you can poach 4-5 thighs in some water to cover, with carrots and onions added, and then you have stock as well. If you use pork sausage, just brown and drain a pound of it and set it to the side until it's time to add it.

You will need some spices you may not have in your pantry, like sage and poultry seasoning, as well as onions, bell pepper, celery, chicken broth, and eggs. And a 9x13 casserole pan, but this dish halves nicely, and then you can make it in an 8-inch cast-iron skillet.

Start off by preheating your oven to 350 degrees, then crumble your cornbread into a big bowl. If you ignored me and made cornbread today for this occasion, then scatter it on a cookie sheet and toast it for 30 minutes at 200 degrees to dry it out. I can't overemphasize that the cornbread you use needs to be dry. Dressing was how our forebears used up scraps.

Toast three pieces of sandwich bread and crumble it, too, tearing the pieces into tiny bits the size of the end of your finger. Stir it into the cornbread.

Then take a large, preferably cast iron, skillet and put a couple of tablespoons of whatever oil you use—butter, olive, corn — in it, and then add a cup of diced onion, a cup of diced bell pepper, and a cup of diced celery and sauté it until the onions become transparent and the peppers get tender. We are probably talking about 7-10 minutes over medium heat. If you are fancy, you can do half a cup of red peppers and half a cup of green, but mostly we used what we could get cheap, which was usually green.

When the vegetables are tender, pour them into the bowl with cornbread crumbles, and stir them in. Now, whatever meat you are using, this is where you add it to the bowl and stir it in, too.

Where most people mess up their dressing is, they make it too dry. You need a lot of chicken broth to make this work—I say at least four cups, maybe five if your bread is really dry. Add it to the cornbread bowl slowly, a half a cup, and then stir, another half a cup and then stir, continued until it is "right."

The right texture takes time to recognize. Still, a proxy for experience is the texture of the cornbread after you added the broth: If you took up a handful of crumbs and tried to make a ball with it, would it fall apart and be crumbly? Then it's too dry. Would it ooze away like pancake batter? Then it's too wet. Ideally, you want it wet enough that if you formed a ball with it, the ball would hold its shape, but barely.

Another place where people mess up is in not properly seasoning their dressing. This is a very "sage-forward" dish. There is the sage you add, then the poultry seasoning also has sage in it, and if you use breakfast sausage, it probably has sage as well. Or at least it should. To the bowl of cornbread mixture, add a heaping tablespoon of sage, and then stir it in. Then, a heaping tablespoon of poultry seasoning and stir it in. Finally, add two teaspoons of black pepper and, you guessed it, stir it in.

Taste it and see if it needs salt. I am an under-salter, figuring it is easier to add it than to take it away, but it should taste pretty much as you expect it to right now. Add salt if you need to, and then finally, take two eggs, beat them, and then stir them into the mixture. The egg's main purpose is to hold everything together.

Spread it into a greased 9x13 pan, smoothing the top of it out with a spatula. Greasing the pan with a stick of butter was always my job as a child, but these days I usually just hit it with Pam. Fatigue makes cowards of us all.

Pop it in the oven for 45 minutes and then allow it to cool. I've never had it served hot—this is ideally served at room temperature, with gravy of some type poured over the top or with the cranberry sauce I shared with you elsewhere in these pages.

And while it might seem like a lot of work, it really isn't. Chopping an onion, some celery, and a bell pepper. Shredding some cooked chicken. Planning ahead and freezing some extra cornbread when you make a batch. Properly prepared, you could have this as a main course for supper any night of the week.

You deserve it.

Southern cornbread

Note: *I have replicated this recipe here from chapter three for your convenience. To make Chicken and Dressing, you need two batches of this, ideally made at least a day before. You can make them together in a 12-inch cast-iron skillet (or, in an emergency, in a 9x13 cake pan), or individually as detailed below. – HH*

Ingredients

- 1 cup cornmeal, either yellow or white

- 1 tsp baking powder

- 1/2 tsp salt

- 1 cup buttermilk

- 1 large egg

- 2 tablespoons of butter or margarine

- 1 8 to 10-inch well-seasoned cast-iron skillet or, if your life
  is not going well, a cake pan

Preheat the oven to 450. Put butter in a cast-iron skillet and then put the skillet in the oven to melt.

Mix the dry ingredients in a bowl and then add the egg and buttermilk to the dry stuff and mix with a spoon until the batter has an even consistency. Remove the skillet (be careful, it's hot!), swirl the melted butter all over the skillet, then pour the melted butter into the batter.

Stir the batter once to incorporate the butter, then pour the batter into the skillet, and jiggle it so the batter is evenly distributed.

Put it in the oven until it's done: it will be golden brown on top, the sides will pull away from the side of the skillet, and a knife blade comes out dry from the center. For an 8-inch skillet, this takes about 20 minutes; a 10-inch one, about 17.

Chicken and Dressing

Ingredients

- A double batch of Southern Cornbread

- 2 tablespoons of oil – olive, butter, or corn are all fine

- 1 cup diced celery

- 1 cup diced onions

- 1 cup diced bell peppers – feel free to mix colors up if you
  feel festive

- 2 cups shredded cooked chicken or 1 pound pork breakfast sausage

- 3 slices of sandwich bread, toasted and shredded

- 1 teaspoon black pepper

- 1 tablespoon sage

- 1 tablespoon poultry seasoning

- 4-5 cups of chicken broth

- 2 eggs, beaten

- Salt

Preheat the oven to 350 F. In a large bowl, crumble the cornbread and set aside.

Add the oil to the skillet and set over medium heat. Sauté the celery, onions, and bell pepper until the onions are translucent and the peppers are tender.

Stir the vegetables, chicken, and breadcrumbs into the cornbread, mixing well. Add enough chicken broth until the mixture forms a wet ball (see note). I find I use 4 cups, or sometimes a bit more.

One at a time, stirring each one in well, add sage, black pepper, and poultry seasoning. Add salt if needed. Then stir the eggs into the mixture, combining well, and then spread it into a well-greased 9x13 pan. Bake for 45 minutes, remove and serve at room temperature.

18

CHOSEN FAMILY

Our friends Karen and Toney are retired jewelers, and they have had a life full of adventures. As a result, they have a wide range of friends from all over the world. And when we lived in their city, so far from our own families, they sort of adopted us. A mutual friend once said that Karen and Toney collect people. And we were part of their collection.

They lived in a large old house filled with knick-knacks from their travels—there is the Persian rug brought back from Iran, over there the Buddha from India, the animal skin from the Southwest, the antique couch from Goodwill. It was an eclectic house, but a happy one too.

And when we lived there, we went to their house for Thanksgiving. Everyone brought something, and just as their friends were eclectic, so was the meal—there was American-style turkey and dressing, for sure, but there was also baba ganoush, and egg rolls, and empanadas, and baklava. They would put out the invitation—if you don't have a place to eat Thursday, well, now you do. Come as you are and bring what you can.

When you arrived, the table was already full, but Karen always said, "Don't worry—we will make room," and another chair magically appeared, people would scooch their chairs, and now there was room for one more person at this most unlikely of feasts. By the end of the day, there would be several tables added to the end of the dining room table, which now extended into the living room.

And I am here to tell you that would be the best meal you had all year, and the most diverse. The last year we were there we ate with, among others, a house painter, a professional dulcimer player, a nurse who worked on death row, a Syrian mathematician, a folk singer, and the woman who had worked the front desk at a nearby retirement community.

It was crowded, and there was lots of shuffling and "pardon me" and "let me scooch by". There were kids playing and new people arriving and hugs and introductions and passing the potatoes and the desserts—my God, the desserts.

And after the meal, the musical instruments would come out, and impromptu jam sessions would happen, and people who had other obligations would come by to visit. Their daughter's ex-husband was a vegetarian, and since he often had to work on Thanksgiving he would come by during this point, and Karen had always made sure there was food he could eat, and a plate would be made and his children would surround him as he ate, and tell him of their adventures that day.

And it would last until late in the evening, with people snacking the rest of the day, and guitar picking in the living room and camera flashes and...

It was always a very good day.

But we also got invited to birthday parties. Dance recitals. Block parties. Christmas. Easter. It was lovely—we were part of their family. You instantly had plans for every holiday; you had people who loved you; you had people who would miss you when you moved away. And people you miss since you moved away.

It seems to me that there are two types of family: those you are born into, and those you choose. And while the former is a biological fact, the second is a decision.

19

THE BLACKBERRIES

When he was still a child, the world lost its mind, and he lied about his age to go into the Army. I don't know, at this great distance, what led to that decision—he died before I knew to ask such questions, and he was never much for talking about his inner-life, anyway, so no one I ever could ask knew.

It was the second decade of the last century, and the entire world was at war, and this teenage boy, always large for his age, would end up as a pilot, flying planes that had open cockpits and required scarfs and goggles and he would do things nobody should ever have to do and would see things nobody in his hometown had ever dreamed about.

Later, after the war was over, he would return to the States, travel with an air show for a while as a barnstormer, and eventually settle down in North Texas, marry my great-grandmother, and have some kids. My mother's father was his oldest son.

He was a large man, about 6'5", barrel-chested and thick. He wore bib overalls and work shirts and had hands the size of canned hams. He was larger than life in so many ways, not just his size, and he captured all my attention, with his cows and border collies and his 1946 pickup he called "Smooth Mouth" that had lost both third gear and reverse, so driving it took some planning.

He was my great-grandfather, but that was a mouthful for a young feller like me, so I called him Big Un.

We didn't really have money for vacations when I was a child, so we visited family instead. Every summer, around the Fourth of July, we would make the eight-hour trip to North Texas and stay with my grandfather in that magical world where we milked cows in the morning and the pickup trucks had names.

On this summer day in 1976, my great-grandmother and I had been blackberry picking. We sprayed ourselves down with Deet to scare away the chiggers and took empty coffee cans and walked through the pasture to the fencerow where the wild blackberries were rampant. It was there that we filled our cans and our mouths and black juice ran down my face and all the while she told me things I cannot remember, but the thing I do remember is how safe and loved I felt, and how lucky I must be to belong to people that owned both cows and blackberry bushes.

I no longer recall (if I ever knew) where she went that day, but she told Big Un that when she returned, she was going to make a blackberry cobbler with those berries for dessert.

She was not gone for more than a handful of minutes when he called me into the kitchen. They lived in a tiny North Texas farmhouse, with a utilitarian kitchen with cracked linoleum on the floor, a 1950s era Formica and stainless-steel table, and an electric icebox in the corner that now contained, among other things, a 1 pound coffee can full of blackberries so full of goodness they were about to burst.

Big Un put me at the table and put down two mismatched bowls, the porcelain glazing cracked and crazed from years of use. Mine had a faded rose on the bottom of the bowl. The coffee can of blackberries was retrieved from the icebox, and with his huge, rough, scarred hands he poured the blackberries from the can into my bowl and then his. The berries were of various sizes, the way wild berries always are, filling both our bowls to the edge and then he poured the fresh cream we had gotten from his own cows that very morning over the top, the cream running over the berries, filling in the cracks and crevices until the berries looked very much like small blue-black islands in a sea of creamy white.

We sat there, he and I, in a four-room house in North Texas, 70 years and a Formica table between us, quietly eating the purloined blackberries. When she came back, there would be hell to pay, and no cobbler to eat, but for now, we were content to merely be together, eating our berries and certain in the knowledge that no king had never had it so good.

Blackberry cobbler

My people made three or four different kinds of cobbler, mostly involving biscuit dough. And I like those. I really do. But I also like this quick cobbler that we often doubled and took to potlucks. - HH

Preheat the oven to 350 degrees.

Ingredients
- ½ cup of flour

- ½ cup of sugar

- ½ cup of milk

- 1 tsp of baking powder

- ¼ tsp of salt

- 2 cups of fresh or thawed blackberries*

Mix all the dry ingredients in a medium-sized bowl, and then stir the milk into it. It will form a thin batter. Pour the batter into a 9x9 pan (this also works with an 8-inch cast-iron skillet, have you been so blessed as to be the possessor of such a thing). Then pour the fresh fruit on top of the batter, spreading it around to make sure the pan is covered. Bake for 40 minutes.

*You can use most any fruit with this. In the summer when peaches are cheap and our blueberry bushes are bursting with berries, we like to make it with a cup of chopped peaches and a cup of blueberries and call it peachberry cobbler. In the dead of winter, I made it with drained canned peaches. If you use frozen fruit, thaw and drain it first. If you don't properly drain your canned fruit, it will still taste good, but the texture will be different.

20

FIREHOUSE SOUP

While I went to college, I worked for a few years as a firefighter for the City of Memphis.

The deal was that you worked every other day for three days, and then you were off for four days. So, for example, you may work Monday, Wednesday, and Friday, and then you would be off until the following Wednesday, when the cycle started all over again. And each shift was 24 hours long and began at 7 AM. Depending on what fire-fighting equipment was housed at your station, you could have anywhere from four to 12 people on each shift, and you always worked with the same people.

It was like a second family you lived with for a third of your life. We had laundry and chores and we cut the grass and, of course, ate together. And while there was a kitchen and equipment such as pans and knives provided, the actual food was not and was up to you. Some people brought their own food, but you didn't dare if you wanted to be trusted by the others on your shift. To be trusted, you needed to belong to the syndicate.

I worked at several engine houses during the years I was on the job, and the syndicate always worked the same way. There was one member of the shift who kept track of a pool of money, and that was used to buy groceries for your shift. Each shift had its own refrigerator and cupboard, which were kept locked. At each meal, you were "in" or "out" for the meal, meaning you intended to eat the food bought from the pool of money, and you were "charged" your pro rata share of the groceries that went into that meal. And on payday, you settled up your bill, which replenished the pool of money, and it started all over again.

So, every day you worked, you had to figure out who was cooking the three meals for your shift. Some shifts had one person who just loved cooking, and they took it on as their responsibility, but most times we would ask who wanted to cook each meal, with the others doing cleanup. Breakfast was usually fixed—eggs, bacon, biscuits were common, most often with gravy—and lunch was often catch as catch can, but the big show was supper.

A cool thing about this system is that you had a diversity of cooks, with each bringing their favorites to the table. Tom was in his 20s and could run the grill, but not much else. Curtis loved to make spaghetti. Stan made round steak and gravy, with mashed potatoes and English peas so good that my mouth waters just thinking about it.

And John always made soup.

John was nearing retirement after nearly 30 years on the job. He had been divorced for nearly 20 of those years, and most of his off-work meals were sandwiches or diner fare. But his one claim to culinary fame was his soup.

I probably ate it two dozen times and watched him make it half of those times, and it was never done exactly the same way twice. It was more of a technique than a recipe, but what it always was, was good.

As an example, I will share how I usually make it, but everything in this recipe is up for negotiation.

Dice a small onion into small pieces, and dice two cloves of garlic while you are at it. In a large pot, crumble a pound of ground beef, add your diced onions, and sprinkle some salt on top of it all, and then, over medium heat, brown the ground beef. Stir it all around until the meat is no longer pink and the onions are translucent, then add the garlic and let it sweat a bit, but don't, for the love of God, let it burn or you just ruined the whole thing. The garlic will be flavorful and ready in about a minute.

Pour in three and a half cups of beef broth (or water plus an appropriate amount of beef paste) and a 12-ounce can of V8 juice. Using a spoon or something, scrape the bottom of the pan to make sure all the bits are off the bottom of the pan and it's all mixed well.

To this, add a 15-ounce can of diced tomatoes (Rotel is another option here, but it obviously changes the flavor), a couple of tablespoons of Worcestershire sauce (easy for you to say), and 2 teaspoons of Italian seasoning. We had only a few spice jars at the fire station, but Italian seasoning went into everything. Let it come to a boil.

While you are waiting on that, peel and dice two potatoes of whatever kind you have around—I had Yukon Golds. Add it to the pot, along with a pound of frozen mixed vegetables. (I know that sounds vague, but that's what they are always called at the grocery.

It's a premixed bag of green beans, carrots, and English peas.) Let it boil, then bring it down to a simmer for 15 minutes.

NOW. You can let it simmer for another 15 minutes and have a perfectly acceptable soup to serve with your dinner. Or you can do what I do and add a cup and a half of elbow macaroni and another half cup of beef broth and THEN let it simmer for another 15 minutes and have a hearty, filling soup you can eat for dinner all by itself.

Beef or shredded chicken. V8 or tomato sauce. Beef broth or chicken. Macaroni, or spaghetti, or even instant grits (trust me on this). Tomatoes or Rotel. White potatoes or sweet potatoes (What? Yes.)

It's all up in the air. Mix and match. Live a little.

You deserve it.

Vegetable beef soup

Ingredients

- 1 lb. ground beef

- 1 small onion diced

- 1 clove of garlic, minced

- Salt & pepper to taste

- 3 1/2 cups beef broth (homemade, canned, or made with beef base)

- 1 15 oz can of petite diced tomatoes

- 1 12-ounce can of V8 juice

- 2 tsp Worcestershire sauce

- 2 tsp Italian seasoning

- 16 oz of frozen mixed vegetables

- 2 medium-sized potatoes (any variety will do - we use russet)

In a large pot or Dutch oven, add your ground beef, onion, and garlic and cook until the meat is no longer pink and the onions are translucent.

Add your salt and pepper and mix to combine.

Mix in your beef broth, tomatoes, tomato soup, Worcestershire sauce, Italian seasoning, vegetables, and potatoes.

Bring to a boil, then reduce heat, cover, and simmer for about 30 minutes until the potatoes are tender.

21

NO RESPECTER OF PERSONS

Often when reading a novel, if the author wants to indicate the smell of poverty, they will mention the smell of cooked cabbage. Like, "The stairway in the tenement smelled of used diapers, cooked cabbage, and despair."

That's no reflection on the cabbage, however, as cabbage is no respecter of persons, is filled with vitamins, and will keep in your fridge (or in your cellar) for damn near forever. No, besides all the virtues of cabbage, it is also usually inexpensive, which makes it the butt of jokes rather than be celebrated for the heroic vegetable it is, having filled in around the edges when the more respected fare is scarce during that hungry time in late winter, between the put-by food being eaten and the garden not yet producing.

As a young boy, I ate my share of cooked cabbage, but sadly, I had no cooked cabbage that tasted good until I was grown. My people tended to, when in doubt, just boil a thing until it surrendered. We made up for this by pouring the potlikker in the pot's bottom -

the vitamin laden broth left after the cabbage had been eaten - over cornbread, which was always the best part of the meal, the cabbage having been cooked until it dissolved, like the dreams we had of a meal with texture.

But done right, stewed cabbage is a delight, and there is virtually no likker to be had because we didn't soak away all the vitamins. If it's a weeknight and you don't know what to use for a side dish, this is perfect. It takes about 25 minutes from start to back, and if you add some bacon, you can make it a main dish instead. I think it's even good enough to serve as a side at a celebration, like Thanksgiving. If stewed cabbage is wrong, I don't want to be right.

What you will need for this is a head of white cabbage, a big skillet, three tablespoons of some cooking fat - bacon grease is traditional, but butter is OK too, and I like to mix them both, half and half, each bringing qualities of which the other is shy - some salt, some sugar, and some water.

Turn the heat to medium under your skillet and put your fat in it to melt. I'm going to assume you paid attention and are using one and a half tablespoons each of both butter and bacon grease, but you do you. Unless you doing you involves olive oil, in which case, just … no. There are things for which olive oil is wonderful, but this is not one of them.

While your fat's melting, quarter your head of cabbage, cut out the stem, and then cut the rest of it into "steaks", top to bottom (like, from pole to pole of the cabbage head) about an inch and a half thick. Then cut the steaks into chunks about 2x2 and then put the chunks in the hot fat. Don't shred your cabbage - this is not slaw. You want chunks. It may fall apart a bit, which is fine, but don't encourage it any. I mean, you fall apart, and we do you the kindness of not mentioning it, so return the favor here.

Sprinkle a tablespoon of sugar and a teaspoon of salt over the cabbage chunks. You want to give the cabbage a minute or two in the hot fat, so the leaves will begin to brown and caramelize - take your spatula and move it about a bit to keep it from sticking. When you see edges beginning to brown slightly, add a cup of water (slowly), and then allow the water to cook down over medium heat until the water is mostly gone, the house smells amazing, and the cabbage is tender when you stab it, but the chunks are still mostly intact - which on my stove takes about 20 minutes.

Some of you will want to cook this for longer. I understand this, but you are wrong. It won't be improved by turning it into mush. I am in favor, however, of starting this dish by frying up three slices of bacon, then dicing the cooked bacon into bits, and using that bacon grease plus another tablespoon or two of butter as the fat and then proceed from there, using the bacon bits as a garnish when you are done.

Some of you will think this can be improved by reducing the fat down to only one tablespoon, making it less fattening. It may be less fattening that way, but it won't taste better and, in fact, will be embarrassing if you serve it to people who love you. And in all honesty, two tablespoons of butter have 200 calories, which when divided by the four servings this makes, means you saved 50 calories a serving, but turned something delicious into something your kids will mock you for making.

Stewed cabbage

Ingredients

- 1 medium head of cabbage

- 1 and 1/2 tablespoons of bacon grease

- 1 and 1/2 tablespoons of butter

- 1 teaspoon of salt

- 1 tablespoon of sugar

- 1 cup of water

Put a large cast-iron skillet on medium heat, then add butter and bacon grease.

Remove the outer leaves, then core the cabbage and cut it into chunks, approximately 2x2x1 inches. DO NOT SHRED. Place them in the hot fat, then sprinkle salt and sugar over the top of the cabbage chunks. Allow to cook for a minute or two until the cabbage starts to brown - you may have to turn the heat down a bit. Nudge the cabbage chunks periodically to avoid sticking. When edges begin to brown, SLOWLY pour a cup of hot water into the pan, then allow it to cook down until the cabbage is tender and the water is 90% gone. This will take ~ 20 minutes. Do not overcook.

22

TREATING YOURSELF LIKE FAMILY

My dad taught me to cook. Or rather, he made sure I knew how. But he didn't teach me to like it. Spenser did that.

But I am getting ahead of myself.

I have spent many words in these pages to make the connection between food and love. But I wasn't taught that—that came later. In our house, food was utilitarian. It provided nutrition, and while we had favorites that Mom cooked, I don't know that she ever experienced anything like joy in making it. To Dad, being able to cook meant you could take care of yourself and others, so he made sure I knew how. His own father had died when he was seven, leaving him and his mom alone and unsure how to navigate the world without him. For Dad, being able to cook was about survival.

As I have related elsewhere, I did not enjoy my teenage years. I was smarter than most of the people I knew, and they knew it. I loved Shakespeare and poetry. However, in almost every way that proficiency was measured in Independence, Mississippi, I was terrible. I could not play sports, I did not hunt, and I did not have a fast car or a hot girlfriend.

In the summer I turned sixteen, I discovered the writing of Robert B. Parker. Parker wrote detective fiction—in fact, some say he saved the detective novel from disappearing—and his detective was named Spenser. No first name. (If you are of a certain age, you may have seen the derivative TV show called *Spenser for Hire*, but we do not speak of that here.)

Spenser lived in Boston, was a former boxer and an ex-cop. He was tough, like you expect a detective to be, but he also quoted poetry and knew something about what wine to drink with dinner. He was a smart-ass, but also a Boston liberal in his politics. He was everything I needed.

Living in a small house on 40 acres in Mississippi, I only had one sort of role model. But Spenser showed me a different world. It was from Spenser that I heard the first argument for abortion I found compelling. It was from Spenser that I first met gay characters in a novel, and they weren't freaks, but good folks. It was from Spenser that I was introduced to (a mild form of) feminism. And it was from Spenser I learned about Thoreau.

In one of the books, *Promised Land*, Spenser said tha he believed most of the nonsense Thoreau was preaching, and that he had spent a long time getting to where he could live life on his own terms.

The next day I was in the school library, looking for Thoreau, which led me to *Walden*, which consumed me that year. It began a love affair for me that hasn't ended, 30 years later. I realized that this autonomy thing, the way I am wired, belonged to *a tradition*. I wasn't a freak. I belonged.

My absolute favorite book of Parker's was *Early Autumn*. Paul, a boy in his teens, who is socially awkward and who does not fit in, is a major character in the story. His mother hires Spenser to protect him from his father, who she fears will kidnap him. Spenser learns neither parent loves Paul—he is just a pawn in their hatred of each other. Paul is failing to thrive because no one has taught him how to move in the world. So Spenser sort of adopts him and teaches him how to be.

That is how I felt—I did not know how to be in the world, and Spenser showed me the way. Just like he did Paul.

Spenser taught me to embrace my judgement. To credit my opinion. Being a smart-ass was an acceptable choice when you didn't know what else to do. I lifted weights because Spenser did. I studied poetry in college because Spenser did. I learned how to fight, like Spenser did. I learned to develop my own code of conduct, to worry about things like being honorable and fighting for the underdog. And I learned to love to cook.

Spenser can cook. That is one of his things. It is one way he maintains his space in the world.

In another book, which I can't find to quote at the moment, Spenser explains that knowing how to cook is not only a means of survival, but a way to take control, and to be kind to yourself. He says that by cooking an enjoyable meal, by setting the table, he is treating himself like a family. He also has a line to the effect that there is nothing sadder than a grown man leaning against the counter in his kitchen eating cold Chinese takeout.

So, I embraced it. I learned to cook and to cook well. I took it seriously, because while I had always known that eating together was a sign of love, I came to know that cooking good food, even when I was the only one there to eat it, was a sign of love for myself. I came to see cooking as a creative act, the creation of an ephemeral piece of art that if you screw up, you get to erase (or eat, if it isn't too bad) and try again tomorrow.

But most importantly, I learned to treat myself like family.

23

FROM THE PANTRY

I believe in having a certain amount of food on hand. Two to three months' worth of regular, everyday food, that is; not dehydrated tofu you keep in a bunker out back.

This might lead you to believe I am some sort of doomsday prepper, but after the supply chain shortages of recent years, I just feel like I am a realist. Another benefit of having a deep pantry is that it gives you the ability to create a good dinner quickly without leaving the house.

Tonight, I came home, and it was 5:30, and I realized I had forgotten to set anything out to thaw for supper, and what's worse, I had forgotten that I had a meeting at 7 I couldn't miss.

So, I looked in the pantry for inspiration and saw a couple of potatoes that were in danger of going bad, so I needed to do something with them. We have chickens, so we always have eggs on hand. But even if I didn't have chickens, eggs last a really long time, much longer than you think, in the fridge. So, I pretty much always have lots of eggs on hand. And we always have lots of canned and frozen vegetables.

So, I peeled the two potatoes and then sliced them on the mandolin about a ¼ inch thick. I took down a 10-inch nonstick skillet and put it on medium heat and then added a tablespoon of olive oil to it. Now, you could use any fat here—butter freezes like a dream, by the way, and I probably have 10 pounds of it in the freezer and there is always a jar of bacon grease in the door of my refrigerator—but I like the flavor of olive oil on potatoes and I have a bottle that lives on the counter by the stove.

Take the potato slices and place them in the oil so they overlap and cover the entire bottom of the skillet. Add a generous portion of salt and pepper. Again, here is a place you could make changes—I have used a big shake or two of Creole seasoning here, or seasoning salt, or, like I did tonight, just salt and pepper. It all depends on what sort of mood you are in.

I like chicken stock and make it when I have bones to use up, but for things like this, I just keep a jar of the good bouillon base in the fridge (and another, unopened one, in the pantry). Before I peeled the potatoes, I had turned on the electric kettle that lives on our counter, and so I added one teaspoon of chicken base to one cup of boiling water and whisked the hell out of it to get the base to dissolve. I then pour the cup of stock in the skillet and partially cover it, letting it simmer for a few minutes.

While it's simmering, I open a can of whole kernel corn and reserve the liquid, but then dump the corn in the skillet, spreading it around so there is a layer of corn on top of the potatoes. By now, the potatoes should get soft and the liquid boiling away, but if it is boiling away too fast and your potatoes are not yet soft, then add some of the corn broth to the skillet for the additional liquid you need. If they are softening fine, keep it going until the chicken broth has mostly boiled away.

What you are going for here—and it will take you somewhere between 10 and 15 minutes—is for the potatoes to be soft, and for the liquid to be 90% gone.

While it's cooking away, get out 5 eggs, and scramble them with a whisk until smooth. Then either shred some cheddar cheese or, if you found some on sale cheaper than the block of un-shredded cheddar, get out a half cup of shredded cheese. (As an aside, if you get a bunch of pre-shredded cheese, it also freezes well and still works for the things it is good for, like this.) Now trust me on this-mix the cheese into the eggs.

Now your potatoes should be soft, and the liquid mostly cooked away. Before the next step, turn your broiler on high and let it warm up. Next, lift the skillet and shake it gently, checking the potatoes aren't sticking. Then pour the egg and cheese mixture over the contents of the skillet. Then take a spatula and gently lift the edges of the potatoes, so the egg mixture slips amongst the potatoes.

After it has begun to set, constantly move your spatula around under the edges so it doesn't stick, then slide the skillet six inches under the broiler and let the top of the egg mixture cook and bubble until it turns the lightest version of brown. Pull it out and set it on a trivet to cool while you set the table, then cut it into four wedges. It actually plates up better if you let it cool 10 or 15 minutes before you serve it, but I often eat it hot and let the plate be a little messy. I put hot sauce on top of mine tonight, but sometimes do chow-chow or salsa instead.

The worldly among you will recognize this is a sort of frittata if you are Italian, or a tortilla if you are Spanish. I ate them for years without knowing they were European. This will serve two people for supper, or four people for lunch. It's free of meat but has 44 grams of protein, and if you used vegetable broth or juice from the can of corn instead of chicken broth, it would be full-on vegetarian and, of course, it's gluten-free. And it only messed up one skillet and a bowl to scramble the eggs in, only took 20 minutes from start to finish to make, and I didn't even have to have a plan.

Pantry frittata

Ingredients

Preheat the broiler to high

- 2 tablespoons of olive oil

- Two potatoes

- 1 cup of chicken stock

- 1 can whole kernel corn

- Salt and pepper to taste

- 5 eggs

- ½ cup shredded cheese (I like cheddar for this)

Slice the potatoes thin (a mandolin works well here).

In a large nonstick skillet over medium heat, add the olive oil, and then layer the slices of potato in the oil. Let them brown for a few minutes and add salt and pepper.

After 3-4 minutes, add one cup of chicken stock and one can (drained) of whole kernel corn (reserve the broth from the corn). Cover the skillet partially and allow the stock to simmer and reduce. When the stock is 90% gone, make sure the potatoes are tender to the fork—if not, add some corn broth to the skillet and continue until the potatoes are tender.

With a fork, scramble the five eggs, then add the cheese to the eggs and mix well. Pour the egg and cheese mixture over the potatoes, then using your fork, nudge the potatoes around so the egg mixture can get in and around the potatoes and corn.

Then cook over medium heat, nudging here and there so the egg mixture is well incorporated, until it begins to get firm in the middle. Then, place the skillet under the broiler for 3-4 minutes until the top begins to turn brown.

Best served at room temperature.

24

CHURCH OF THE DINER

A few years ago, I was in Baltimore, a city I have never spent any time in. So, being in a strange town all by myself, I did what I always do—I found a diner to eat breakfast in.

I have eaten in diners in, I believe, 28 states, and even though the diners are all different, they are always the same. In a real sense, they are like churches, with public liturgy, a crowd of regulars, a common text. While there are many choices, we all have our favorites.

You have your 23rd Psalm; I have my ham and cheese omelet with a side of fruit.

Like churches, which are easily identifiable as such by things like steeples and stained glass, there is a common architecture for diners as well: Formica tables and broad expanses of glass facing the street, a counter that serves the single folks, the pot of coffee, the orange juice machine.

The elements of the service are similar from place to place, too. Just like a chalice or altar is immediately recognizable, so also are the thick white China mugs in a diner, perhaps the most perfect device ever invented for consuming coffee. Coffee tastes better from a heavy porcelain mug with a thick lip, and if the server is on it, they will run hot water in it first to warm the mug up, keeping your coffee warmer longer.

In the Church of the Diner, they welcome regulars, but are happy if today is the only time you come in. Unlike most churches I have attended, they welcome newcomers with no expectation that they will ever return. They are content for you to join their community just for today, to take part as much or as little as you want and trust you will leave happier than when you arrived.

"I don't know you or your story, fella, but you look hungry. Come on in," they seemed to have said.

And so, I do.

As a child, I was castigated for bringing an outside book to read during church, but at the Church of the Diner, my book is welcomed, as is my scruffy, unshaven face and my coffee-stained t-shirt.

They were not offended that day in Baltimore when I did not want to be part of the crowd but was instead content to sit in the corner with my book, drinking coffee and periodically staring out the rain-streaked window as the world came alive.

I have long thought that diners are one of the last bastions of egalitarianism left in this country. The judge will sit in a booth next to a plumber, who sits in the booth next to an unhoused man who is buying his coffee with spare change given him by a kind soul.

As I looked around, I wasn't proven wrong. The other diners are diverse. There is a shift-worker eating a meal before heading home. At the counter, a sex-worker was drinking coffee. A table of rowdy folks in their early twenties haven't made it home yet after a Saturday night out. A collection of old men sit at a corner table, flirting with the server and occasionally laughing a bit too loud—a scene you feel has happened daily for years.

Everyone is welcome at the church of the diner.

At a diner near my old house in Raleigh, a server passed away suddenly. I did not really know her—she had waited on me several times, and we passed the time of day, but at diners I am often just the observer, sitting in the corner with a book, listening to the ambient chatter, soaking in the presence of other, so I did not really know her the way other regulars did.

On the counter near the cash register was a picture of her, a candid snapshot downloaded from her Facebook profile, because who has actual paper photos of anyone these days? And in the weeks after her death, a jar sat there, taking up a collection for her funeral expenses. I always added my change in the jar, and sometimes, an additional 5 or 10-dollar bill. After all, in the Church of the Diner, we take care of our own.

There are faded newspaper clippings on the wall near the cash register: obituaries of regulars, commendations received by police officers who are regulars, a spelling bee victory by the kid who comes in with their parents.

Like any church, they have their nut jobs. The people who can't make it through the day without a drink, the people who take advantage of community to hustle and scheme. The annoying person who won't leave you alone when it is obvious you want to be left alone. Amazingly, there are diner fanatics as well.

There is a woman who regularly came into a diner I used to frequent. I was there once or twice a week, at random times, and she was there fully 50% of the time. She knew all the servers' names and had the menu memorized. She had, a server told me, been coming in for years and had applied to work there many times and never got called in for an interview. But she was undaunted and kept coming back. I don't know what she was looking for, but I feel that way about church sometimes, too.

A mentor once told me that communities eat together, celebrate together and mourn together. Come to think of it, he told me that while we were sitting in a diner.

25

AN ACT OF SELF-LOVE

Myfather was seven years old on that bitterly cold February day when his father had a heart attack. In those days, there was no ambulance for poor folks who didn't live in town, so my grandmother called the funeral home, and they took him to the hospital in the hearse.

Dad said it was snowing when he was told his father had died. He never did much care for snow after that. His death left my grandmother, a 47-year-old woman who had outlived two husbands, in charge of a house, 40 acres, and a 7-year-old boy. She had no skills considered valuable by the marketplace. She couldn't even drive a car when he died.

Dad was forced to grow up fast, and when he had children of his own, he lived in terror that he too would die early, leaving us to fend for ourselves. It was his mission to make sure we were better prepared than he had been on that snowy day in February.

Which is how Dad and I ended up in the kitchen that morning. I was 7 years old—the same age he had been when his own father died. Since Dad was making breakfast, it must have been a Saturday morning. Dad could cook, within narrow limits, and he enjoyed doing it. His biscuits were things of beauty. He pan-broiled his bacon, not having the patience to cook the slices individually. And on that morning, he taught me how to scramble eggs.

"If you know how to cook eggs and make toast, you never, ever have to be hungry and can always take care of yourself."

I was 30 years old and a failure in every way anyone measured. I had married a rich man's daughter, had been heir apparent at the family firm, and then walked away from it all. During my final year at the firm, I earned $96,000. The following year I would make $18,000 and live in a friend's attic apartment with a leaky roof.

Nobody tells you how long the nights are when you divorce. At work during the day, you can stay busy. But after you get home to your quiet house and sit in your quiet living room, the emptiness of it all hits you.

I would fix myself something to eat - often just a sandwich or a can of soup- stare at the walls and eventually drift off to sleep. In fact, thinking back, a proxy for my mental health is how well I am eating. If I'm eating convenience food, it's often because I just don't have the energy to create something. But it's a downward spiral after that because eating too much convenience food robs me of a creative outlet, which then depresses me, so I feel even worse.

Cooking for yourself is an act of self-care, an act of self-love.

Often during those years, I would wake up in the middle of the night and I would stare at the ceiling, and all the day's problems would be magnified. There are no insignificant problems at 3 AM.

Sometimes I would get up and read until I got sleepy and then try again. But on other nights, sleep would not come. It was on those nights that I would go to CK's.

CK's Coffee Shop was a small chain of steak and egg diners in Memphis that closed years ago. They were Formica-tabled joints with dark wood paneling and jukeboxes. If you are trying to picture them in your head, imagine a Waffle House, but not as nice.

They were open 24 hours a day, and I would go in at three in the morning or so, having given up on sleep and resigning myself to just being up now. The one by my house had an older Black lady who was the sole employee—server, host, cook, busboy - most nights I showed up. The small dining room was always empty at that hour, and I ordered a cup of coffee, a ham and cheese omelet, and toast.

I would sit in the shelter of that dimly lit diner, listen to sad songs on the jukebox, and watch the city come to life. The shift workers coming in when they got off at 4 AM, the cops who would pop in to write their reports before going off shift, the sex workers looking for a break and coffee between clients.

After a while, having finished my eggs and toast, and having drunk many cups of coffee and watched the city come to life, I would head off to work for another day.

The best omelet maker I have ever seen with my own two eyes was not my dad, whose omelets were serviceable but unremarkable.

Neither were they those from that solitary nighttime employee at CK's, whose primary virtue was that she showed up for work every night and kept my coffee cup filled.

On the Internet, you can watch Jacques Pepin, who is classically trained and was once the President of France's personal chef, make a bomb-ass omelet in two different variations in less than six minutes, while talking to you the whole time. It is a marvel to behold. He is, as far as I'm concerned, the expert on omelets.

But the best omelet maker I have ever seen in person was in a hospital cafeteria.

My wife was in the hospital for 10 days following heart transplant surgery. For three days, she was in a coma. For those 10 days, I lived at that hospital and slept on a small cot in the corner of her room. The days seemed endless, and there was a coffee shop in the lobby where I would sit, and other times I would read books in the hospital's meditation garden, just to pass the time.

And I ate every meal in the cafeteria.

This goddess of the griddle arrived every morning at five AM and opened the short-order station, where one could have eggs or sausage or bacon and, pertinent to this essay, you could get an omelet cooked to order right in front of you.

My order was always the same for those ten days: ham, cheese, and mushrooms. She had an 8-inch nonstick skillet that soap never touched - after each omelet, she would wipe it clean with a towel and go again.

Once you ordered, she would immediately put the skillet over the fire to warm, and then she would plop a handful of diced ham and sliced mushrooms on the grill in a pile and squirt of what looked like melted butter but was probably some sort of hydrolyzed oil product.

While that was cooking down, she would then put a squirt of the ersatz butter in the skillet and twist the skillet back and forth until the bottom of the skillet had a generous sheen of fat on it.

Into the now hot skillet, she lovingly ladled a scoop of pre-scrambled eggs from a container, which she then quickly coated the entire surface of the bottom of the skillet with by twisting her wrist, in much the same way someone would make a crepe. It was incredibly thin and light, with lace at the edges. She then took her turner and scooped up the ham and mushroom mix from the griddle and, with a flip of her wrist, spread it on the part of the omelet furthest from the handle. Then she placed a slice of American cheese on top of the ham and mushrooms and then slid the entire thing onto a plate, folding the uncovered portion onto the covered side in a deft flip of the wrist. It was 90 seconds max from the time you ordered.

It wasn't the best omelet I have ever eaten, but it was the best made. It was a thing of beauty and precision. Watching her was artistry itself. And every morning for 10 days, I ate her omelets for breakfast. First, as I was filled with dread, and then as my wife's prospects increased, so did the hopefulness I brought to that cafeteria with me. I was going to be OK.

Time and again, eggs have seen me through hard times. Not just economically hard times, although that is also true. An omelet - even a fantastic omelet made from free-range organic eggs from chickens that have names - is usually less than a dollar and a half of ingredients and can be much less than that. But also, eggs lend themselves to the sort of quick, low-mess cookery that our souls cry for when we don't have the energy to go on.

For people in low circumstances—whether economic or emotional or both - eggs can help to create a margin between where we are and where we need to be.

And they are fast. You can go from the idea of an omelet to food on the table in less than five minutes. It takes longer to clean up afterward than it does to make one.

Throughout this book, I have maintained that the act of cooking for those we love and sharing a meal with people we love helps that love to grow.

Somewhere along the way, I learned it was OK to love myself and to treat myself like a loved one. I cook for myself—even when I don't feel like it—because I deserve it. I am worthy of it, and it is an act of self-care and self-love to treat myself like a loved one.

When I feel like my mental state is going south, one way I intervene to change my condition is to make myself something to eat.

Not just for the fuel, but for the experience of taking various ingredients and make them into something new, to bring order to the chaos, to treat myself to something I like, to told myself I am worth the trouble, to have something tangible at the end of the process that I can point to and say "I did that!", and to remind myself that there are things (like cooking) that I am really, really good at.

You need little gear to make yourself (or someone else!) a fantastic omelet, but I recommend you get a quality non-stick skillet. Don't spend too much money here, as they all wear out eventually and are thus disposable. I find that if I buy a heavy aluminum one and only use it for eggs and never use metal utensils on it, I will get seven or eight years out of it. The 8-inch size is perfect for up to three eggs or one serving. If you want to make omelets for more than one person, they are fast enough that you can make them one at a time, or you can make one large omelet in a larger skillet and then cut it into wedges, like a quesadilla.

But mostly, in my house, cheese omelets are just for me.

A note to purists: There are multiple variations of omelets around the world. Many cultures have some sort of flat egg dish with stuff in it. For example, there is the tortilla de patatas of Spain, the frittata of Italy, and the omelet of France. There is also the omelet of the US, which shares little other than the name and the ingredients with the omelet of France.

I am not afraid of other egg dishes, and even discuss one at length elsewhere in this book, but this is not that. When I need the comfort of a hot meal that costs me naught but pennies and seconds, I make a diner-style, all-American omelet.

Put your nonstick skillet on the stove over medium heat. Plop a tablespoon (or so) of butter in the skillet and get everything else ready as it melts. It won't take long.

You will need salt, pepper, three eggs, and a 1/4 cup of shredded cheddar cheese.

Break three eggs into a bowl. I have made this with factory-farmed generic .99 cents a dozen eggs and with six-dollar-a-dozen free-range eggs, and either way, it's always wonderful. I'm not the one buying your groceries, but I am a firm proponent of buying the best food you can afford. This nourishes both you and the farmer who produced it.

Add a pinch of salt and pepper, stab the yolk of each egg with a fork, and then whisk it heavily until it is a creamy, gelatinous, well-mixed mess. If you are feeling decadent, you can pour a splash of heavy cream in here before you whisk, but it doesn't require it.

By now, your tablespoon of butter has melted, or mostly so. Twist the skillet around to coat the bottom of the pan and then return it to the heat. Pour your eggs into the skillet and then tilt the pan back and forth to coat the bottom of the pan.

Using a non-metal spatula, lift the edges of the omelet as you tilt the pan, so the runny part runs under the cooked part and comes in contact with the hot skillet. This is fast-paced - it will all be set in 30-45 seconds. The center of the egg mixture should still be damp but not runny. The edges should be set.

Now, some of you are in trouble at this point because you didn't use enough butter. A few of you, God help you, ignored everything I said and used something out of a spray can. You must use enough butter in this, or it will stick. You should be able to slide your omelet around the pan. If not, bang it on the stove and then try. Seriously, bang your skillet to loosen the egg. As a last resort, put your spatula under the eggs and sort of lift them off the pan, and then they should slide around.

Sprinkle a handful of shredded cheddar over the side of the omelet opposite the skillet's handle. Holding the skillet with your right hand with your palm-up, slide the entire thing onto a plate, folding the uncovered portion onto the covered side. (If this makes no sense to you, put the book down, go into the kitchen, and try the gesture with a skillet with nothing in it. The palm-up grip is the easiest way to plate an omelet). The heat of the omelet will finish melting the cheese, and while the outside may have some light brown spots, it should not be brown overall.

This is but a template; there are dozens of ways to make this your own. For example, you can use a spoonful of cottage cheese instead of cheddar. Or any cheese, really. If you don't want to mess up the cheese grater, you can use a vegetable peeler to make thin slices of any hard cheese instead.

A scoop of salsa as a filling is never amiss. Diced mushrooms sautéed in butter are lovely, as is diced ham done the same way, or even together with the mushrooms. I will also sometimes add cooked peppers and onions or cooked diced tomatoes.

The ingredients change, but what is constant is that because I can make an omelet, I can bring order to chaos for less than the cost of a candy bar, make something beautiful, and always take care of myself.

I think Dad would be proud.

A quick US omelet

Ingredients

- Tablespoon of butter

- salt

- pepper

- 3 eggs

- 1/4 cup shredded cheddar cheese

Put a ten-inch nonstick skillet on the stove, turn the burner to medium heat. Add the butter.

Break 3 eggs in a small bowl, then beat with a fork from side to side, until the mixture is homogenized. Add a pinch of salt and a 1/4 teaspoon of pepper and mix well.

When the butter is melted, tilt the skillet to make sure the bottom is well coated with butter, and then pour in the eggs, tilting the skillet back and forth to make sure the bottom of the skillet is well coated with egg. Using a non-metallic spatula, lift the edges of the egg to allow the still runny mixture to slide under the firm parts, so it is all cooked. When done, the center should be damp but not runny, and the whole thing should be set.

Sprinkle the cheddar cheese on the side of the egg mixture opposite the handle, then slide it onto a plate, folding the un-cheesed side onto the cheese as you go.

26

THE ARRIVAL

My mother's father lived in Cooke County, Texas, 50 miles or so from Dallas. He had retired there after he left the Navy and bought some land just up the road from his own parents. There, he and his second wife, my step-grandmother, plunked down a doublewide trailer with a lean-to addition tacked on the back that was a combination TV room and guest room. What made it a guest room was that was where the foldout couch lived, and so thus where I lived when I stayed with them.

There were times the dual roles of this addition—TV room and guest room—were at odds with each other. God help you if you were tired and wanted to go to bed while *Walker, Texas Ranger* was on. You might as well just settle in because you were going to be there a while.

The annual visit to see them was our default vacation plan—every summer of my childhood we would load up whatever car we drove that year with sandwiches and thermoses of coffee and bags of snacks and we would hit the road to visit Papaw and Granny Pat. Dad would work all day the day we would leave, and then come home and pack and load up the car. They planned our departure to be somewhere around 8 PM, and in those days of 55 MPH speed limits, we would roll into Papaw's around 6 AM.

Dad liked to drive at night when there were three kids in the car because we would rapidly fall asleep and he and mom would take turns driving in relative silence, with the windows down and the cool night and the radio fading in and out of range as you drove west into the night.

I loved those trips. You would sit in the backseat of the station wagon—the passenger side was my favorite because that let me watch the scenery better—from where you could see the landscape change from urban lights to Delta fields, clothed in utter darkness pierced only by lights twinkling in the distance, signifying a lone farmer's home on the far edge of the rice field. You cross the Mississippi River in Memphis, and since the AC never worked on our cars, the windows were down and the bridge framework combined with the Doppler effect to make its own sort of music.

On either side of the bridge, the river rolled under you, but from where you sat, it was just endless darkness on either side. Around Little Rock, I would fall asleep, my resolution to stay awake the whole trip forgotten, and my eyes would surrender. I would wake up when we stopped at the truck stop in Texarkana, where Dad would refill his thermos and I would go to the bathroom. That was the first place I ever saw condom machines in the bathroom, and that led 11-year-old me to look up the words French Tickler in the dictionary. Life before the internet was filled with ignorance for pre-teen children.

But after Texarkana, I was out again and would stay out until not far from their house. We would be on a lonely road, with horse farms on either side of the road, and scrub oaks punctuating the fields to give the livestock shade to rest under on the hot days. And it was that liminal time, neither dark nor dawn, where the brightness can be perceived but it's not yet sunrise, giving everything a honeyed glow.

And we would pull into the driveway and all of us would pile out and Dad would stretch like a cat and Mom would make sure the kids were all up and Papaw would come out onto the patio by the driveway and asked how our trip was and Dad would remark how many hours and minutes it took as if we were in a race, and Papaw would call Mom "Tadpole" and give her a hug and we kids would be swamped with hugs and the attention of his Border Collies and we would take our bags inside.

Granny Pat was already up as well, and they had coffee going, and she would start cooking breakfast, always sausage patties and scrambled eggs and whop-um biscuits and milk gravy. You could smell the sausage as you walked in the house, and the whop-um biscuits would be in a round pan, pushing up on each other, and there were always at least three different kinds of jelly on the table.

On the wall, the old man in the Eric Engstrom print prayed over the bread as we all shared stories. Papaw would tell us how we were incorrect in our thinking, no matter what we were thinking, and then, exhausted, Dad would lie down and take a nap after having been awake for more than 24 hours and 500 miles.

The rest of the trip would vary, but the arrival was always special. They must have set the alarm for enough time to prepare for our showing up in those days before ubiquitous cell phones, back when you just told someone when you would show up and that was it.

And the knowledge that people love you and have missed you and have cooked breakfast to celebrate your arrival? There is no feeling like that in the world.

27

COMFORT AND JOY

I t was cold and crisp, and the breath rose from the mouths of the others as they sang, wispy and smoky, ascending towards heaven as we sang Christmas carols.

The houses were decorated with the multi-colored lights we still used in the early eighties, with enormous bulbs. In the windows, lighted Christmas trees stood out against dark backgrounds, and green wreaths with plastic red berries hung on the door. And in the distance, the sound of over the road trucks on the interstate, carrying goods to the store so we could buy them for gifts.

It was mid-December in 1980, and I was Christmas caroling in the inner city.

Until the year she turned sixteen, my mom was a Navy brat, and they moved from place to place. For a few years in her early teens, they had lived in Memphis, and she had made friends with one of the neighborhood girls.

But now, it was twenty years later, and everyone was grown up and had married and now had children of their own. My mom lived in rural Mississippi, but both Bonita and her parents stayed in the neighborhood, and Mom and Bonita were still friends.

Bonita and her husband had kids roughly my age, and so once a month or so I would be at their house and would run and play in abandoned lots and junked out cars and in drainage runoffs and would pretend I too was a tough inner-city kid and not some wide-eyed rube from the country come to town.

And it was the middle of December, and their church was Christmas caroling, and while I had seen Christmas carolers on TV, I had never done it myself, so my folks signed me up.

It was one of any number of adventures my parents signed me up for because it would be good for me.

Which is why, in this story, I am 10 years old and outside in the chilly night air and my toes are cold, and I am singing songs of comfort and joy both with and to people I do not know.

In my memories, we had been singing for hours, all up and down that neighborhood, but I'm sure it was, at best, 45 minutes. But now we were almost done and were to close out this musical tour by performing at Ms. Ruby's house.

Ms. Ruby was Bonita's mother, and she and her husband lived at the end of the same street Bonita lived on, and she was always smiling, and would give me an enormous hug, and call me baby.

It's hard to convey to people who did not live through it just how different the age before instant communication was. You would just show up at people's houses, unannounced, and maybe they would be home and maybe they wouldn't, and it was not uncommon for you to be in your house, minding your own business, when the doorbell might ring, unexpectedly, and now suddenly you had guests!

So that night, we just showed up at Ms. Ruby's house. Bonita said she was sure they were home, but the house seemed dark as our ragtag band of cheer-bringers walked up the driveway and assumed formation, lifted our song sheets, and caroled away.

We were tired and cold, and my feet hurt from the cold, and my fingers were numb. Our voices did not carry the enthusiasm of earlier in the night, the novelty having long since worn off, and had not the parents who were accompanying us kept pushing, we would have abandoned this event long ago.

But here we were, in front of this small, teal-colored house in the inner city, with a wreath on the door but no lights visible.

Then, a light came on in the back of the house. And then another. And then the front door opened, and there was Ms. Ruby, silhouetted in the doorway, light at her back, hair up in curlers, bathrobe ensuring her modesty.

The porch light came on, and the door opened.

"Who's there?" she asked.

Bonita ran up to the door and explained what was going on, while her mother took us all in, gazing at what was surely a spectacle at this late point in the evening.

Ms. Ruby lit up with a smile.

"I hadn't known y'all were coming, so I had gone to bed early. But come on in."

Bonita explained we weren't staying, and that Ms. Ruby's house was the last one of the night, but Ms. Ruby wasn't having it.

"Bonita, these kids are cold. Just look at poor Hugh there—he's almost blue!" Now, turning to us, "Y'all come on inside and get warm."

And so, we did. Some 12 kids and three or four moms all came into the tiny, over-furnished living room, and we sat in chairs brought in from the kitchen table and others sat on the floor and squeezed onto the couch. Ms. Ruby was a flurry of activity, fluffing pillows and turning on lamps, and then paused, looking at us, hands on hips.

"What y'all need is some hot cocoa. Bonita, come help me in the kitchen!"

And then she turned and, with a swoosh of the hem of her house-coat, swept into the kitchen.

The house was warm—so warm, our nose hairs dried up as we quickly shed coats and scarves. While noises came from the kitchen, we were captivated by all the mementos that covered every hori-zontal surface, the pictures on the walls. And we were all talking and telling stories when Bonita came in from the kitchen, carrying a stockpot in both hands, which she set on the dining table.

Ms. Ruby came in behind her, tray in hand containing mugs, and then, after a return trip to the kitchen, deposited a bag of mini-marshmallows on the table.

I think that might have been the first time in my life I had home-made (i.e., not from a packet) hot chocolate, but maybe not. My people were not big hot chocolate people.

What I know with absolute certainty is that it was the best cup of hot chocolate I have ever had in my life. Every part—holding the heavy warm mug in my cold fingers, the smell of melted marshmallow as I sipped it, the heat of the beverage itself on my aching lips, all in that lovely, overstuffed, house, an unplanned refuge on a cold night, taken in and cared for as unexpected guests.

It was magical.

I still love hot chocolate, and it still feels magical.

While we are here—let's get some terms straight. I use hot cocoa and hot chocolate interchangeably. I'm sure there is a difference, but to my people growing up, there was not.

It is for me a comfort drink. I can be cold and damp and miserable, and give me a cup of hot chocolate and my entire mood changes.

That's why they call it comfort food.

But unlike other comfort foods I have talked about in these pages, this requires almost no planning and relies on things you almost certainly have, or at least should have, in your pantry.

It's just my wife and me, and so we don't make huge batches like Ms. Ruby did that night, all those years ago. But it's still magical when you just make it for two folks. The room is quieter, too.

Here's how I make it these days.

Begin with your mugs—ours are 12-ounce size, and so I fill each mug with whole milk, then pour the milk from the mugs into a medium saucepan. This makes sure you have the right amount of milk, and it saves you from dirtying up a measuring cup. Turn on your range to medium heat, and while the milk warms, measure one tablespoon of cocoa and one tablespoon of sugar into the bottom of each mug. This is the basis for all truly great hot cocoa—equal parts cocoa and sugar.

Now stir the milk so it doesn't scorch. Keep your attention on the milk in the pan. You do NOT want it to boil—rather, you want it to want to boil.

When it starts to shimmer and tiny bubbles form around the edge, that will be just about perfect. If you are a perfectionist and want to bring technology into this, you are looking for about 170 degrees. Just don't let it boil. Turn it down if you have to.

Back to the mugs—besides the cocoa and sugar, add two drops of vanilla and a pinch of your good salt. If things are tight and you are a single salt household, you can use your table salt, but I think flaky kosher is better here. Or maybe I'm just fancy like that.

The next step requires hot water—the hotter the better, but I usually just run the tap until it gets really hot. Measure out a teaspoon of hot water and pour it onto the mixture in the mug. Take a spoon and stir, making a thick, rich chocolate slurry.

Your milk didn't boil, did it? Good.

Now take your very hot (but not boiling!) milk and fill each mug 1/3 of the way full and then stir until the slurry is dissolved, then fill the mugs the rest of the way.

This is where you can introduce goodies into the equation. Some people add whipped cream and, for bonus points, top that off with shaved bits of chocolate or a generous shake of cinnamon. Others are old school like me and just throw a handful of mini marshmallows on top and call it a day. Either way is fine and would be appreciated by any cold eight-year-old boy.

Exceptional homemade hot cocoa

Makes 1 (12-ounce mug)

Ingredients

- 12 ounces of whole milk

- 1 heaping tablespoon of powdered cocoa

- 1 heaping tablespoon of sugar

- a pinch of salt (I like kosher)

- Hot water (hot tap water is fine)

- Vanilla extract, as prescribed by your ancestors, or, if they are silent, two drops.

- Goodies: marshmallows, whipped cream, shaved chocolate, etc.

Pour the cold milk into the mug you will drink out of, filling it to the level you want the finished drink to be. Then, pour the milk into your pan and turn the range to medium heat.

While your milk is heating up, measure one heaping tablespoon each of cocoa and sugar into the bottom of the mug. On top of this, add a small pinch of salt and two drops of vanilla.

Measure 1 teaspoon of hot water and pour it on top of the mixture in the mug. Take a spoon and stir, making a thick, rich chocolate slurry.

When the milk starts to shimmer and tiny bubbles are forming around the edge, that is just about perfect (~170 degrees Fahrenheit).

When the milk is ready, add about a third of the milk to the cup, and stir. Then add the balance and stir.

Add whatever goodies you like and serve.

28

The Joy of August

August is a complicated month in Mississippi. It often contains the worst of the heat, the culmination of a long summer, where one is exhausted from the heat, the humidity, where one longs for the feel of grass under your feet and sunshine on your face, but is so depressed from the cabin fever that comes from desperately seeking shade.

One dare not work outside after 10 AM, and even that late is stretching it. The nights are worse. It won't get below 75 degrees for weeks at a time, and so in the old days, when air conditioning was the province of the wealthy, you slept on top of the bedcovers, with at best a light sheet draped over you, a box fan blowing on you, the droning noise lulling you to sleep with the promise of breeze, if not coolness.

And then there are the other days. They do not last long, but they are a glimpse, a foretaste of fall. Faulkner described it like this:

... in August in Mississippi there's a few days somewhere about the middle of the month when suddenly there's a foretaste of fall, it's cool, there's a lambence, a soft, a luminous quality to the light, as though it came not from just today but from back in the old classic times. It might have fauns and satyrs and the gods and—from Greece, from Olympus in it somewhere. It lasts just for a day or two, then it's gone.

It was always in August that the muscadines came in. Muscadines are a type of grape that grows wild in the Southeast, a native plant whose value the indigenous recognized and then cultivated, so nowadays you have two types: the wild ones that grow in the thickets, and the cultivated varieties bred for production.

We had a stand of muscadines that grew in the 3-acre thicket between us and Doc and Monty's place. These were the wild ones, the grapes smaller than their over bred kin that have been trained to run in mannerly rows and over arbors. These ran in and amongst the trees and the bushes, some vines over 25 feet in length, here and there, like the Holy Spirit, going wherever it chooses.

To be clear, if your livelihood depends on it, you want the strict wire frames and the careful pruning in February and the snooty varieties developed at the land-grant universities. But if you see yourself as part of a greater whole, a piece in a chain that depends and exists because of each other, a body that gleans what the birds and the racoons and the possums left behind because they need to eat too, then you let the muscadines run wild in your thicket, and so on one of the rare nice August mornings you find yourself in that thicket looking for the deep blue/black grapes.

Monty was my first guide into that thicket. It would be early in the morning, perhaps seven or so, which was more of an accommodation to me than it was anything else - she had been up since 4:30. She would spray us both down with the foul-smelling spray that kept the chiggers away, and she would change out of her normal canvas shoes and put on thick ones in order to tromp through the vines and the underbrush. With a straw hat on her head and a plastic bucket in my hands that had originally held ice cream, we set off down the hill, past the pigpen, and into the pin oaks and redcedar in search of the muscadines.

The light changed in the thicket - it was darker, and the birdsong was different there, and you herald the rustle of the small animals in the brush, curious about who had invaded their space, who had come to pick their muscadines. The temperature had dropped at least ten degrees.

She would point out the poison ivy and teach me the difference between it and Virginia Creeper that always grows near it. Creeper has five leaves on a node - like it's waving hello to you like the friend that it is. The humus from the generations of leaves was soft underfoot, and the light filtered through the enormous mulberry tree to make interesting patterns on the ground.

The muscadine vines weaved in and out of it all, purple grapes hanging down from their weight, straining against the lush green vines. Muscadines don't grow in bunches, like European grapes do, but in small clusters of 3-20 grapes. You end up picking them much like you would blackberries, one at a time. This makes picking more difficult, but by the age of six I had already learned that no good thing comes easy.

The vines run up into the trees, and the most beautiful clusters are always just out of reach, but there are plenty in the lower regions. And so, an hour later, as the day begins to heat up, and the sweat is forming tiny rivulets that run between your shoulder blades, you head back up the hill, ice cream bucket full.

Muscadines are tasty but have a very thick skin that makes them a poor choice for table grapes. Instead, you juice them and make jelly. Or at least we did. Some folks make wine from them, but they didn't live in our house.

Back in the house, you would wash the grapes, pulling the stems and odd bits that had traveled with them, and then put them in a large saucepan and just cover them with water. Bring it to a boil and then let it come down to a mild simmer. After about ten minutes of simmering, they will burst from the heat - this is a good thing - and then you take a potato masher and you mash away, just like they were potatoes. You want to get the juice out of them, and the way to do that is to make sure the thick skin has broken on all of them. Let the mashed grape mixture keep simmering for 30 minutes or so and then take it off the heat.

Now, for this next part, you really ought to have what the fancy kitchens call a chinois, and what we called a strainer. It's shaped like a cone (wide part at the top) and has a wooden pestle. You put it over a large bowl, and you pour the mashed up grape mixture in it, and the juice runs through and the pulp is left behind. Then you take the wooden pestle and work it in a circle, mashing the pulp through the strainer, leaving behind basically skins and seeds.

If you don't have this handy bit of kit (they sell them cheap at restaurant supply houses) you can get an approximation by mashing the pulp through a sieve or colander. But the chinois works much better and gets more of the pulp.

Now, the difference between jelly and jam is down to what happens next - basically, jam has pulp, and jelly does not.

You use a lot of bowls in making jelly. You need a colander or sieve, and you put it over a big bowl, and you line it with a bandana or piece of old bed sheet or cheesecloth. If you are fancy, while at the restaurant supply store you bought a jelly bag for about $10, but we never had one of those growing up. I do not know why we had a chinois, for that matter, but we did.

Once you line the colander with your cloth, put it over the bowl, and pour the pulp and juice in it, so the cloth strains it and the juice runs in the bowl and the pulp is left behind. You are making jelly, so you just want juice - no pulp. It needs to drip for a few hours, to make sure you have all the juice. Do NOT, under any circumstances, squish the pulp, trying to get the juice out faster. It won't affect the taste, but it makes the jelly cloudy, and nobody wants that.

When it's finished draining, you will need to get your canning supplies ready. It's simple - you need eight half-pint mason jars, and eight rings and lids. You are also going to need what my people called a kettle, but what is called a stock pot in the stores. If you get one made for canning, it will have a rack for jars in the bottom. You can buy these at places like Walmart, ready-made, for less than $30.

Put your jars in it (without the lids) and then fill it with hot water and bring it to a boil - let it boil for 10 minutes to sterilize the jars, then turn the heat off, but leave the jars in the water.

Another thing you are going to need is a jar lifter. These are like large pliers that you used to pick up hot jars from boiling water - Walmart will have them too. I know I have you buying lots of things, but all of this - chinois, canning kettle, jar lifters - will not cost you $100, and will last you the rest of your life.

The rules about canning things change from time to time as we learn more about bacteria and how they work. So, read the labels on the lids you buy, but the ones I've gotten lately just have you wash them in warm water - you used to have to boil them too. After I wash them off, I put them in a bowl (another bowl!) of very warm water just covering them, near the stove.

You are going to have to have everything ready, because this is going to go fast. Spread a dishtowel on the counter. Lift your jars out of the kettle, pour the water out of them and then, without touching them with your hands, put them on the towel, side by side like soldiers. They are hot, so be careful.

It's time to make the jelly. You only need three ingredients - five cups of juice, six cups of sugar, and one package of pectin - we always used Sure Jell. It comes in 11.75-ounce boxes, and they sell it over by the canning supplies in the grocery store. It comes in several varieties, but you want the one that is clearly labeled "original" on the label.

In a large pan or small stockpot, pour in the 5 cups of juice. Add the Sure Jell to it and stir it in well. Turn up the heat and bring it to a rolling boil. You want it boiling hard. Then, while stirring, pour in the sugar. It's important to keep stirring, because you want all the sugar to melt. This will also kill the boil. When it comes back to a boil, let it boil for just one minute, and then remove it from the heat. Taking a slotted spoon, skim as much of the froth off the top of the jelly as you can.

Now you have to move fast. Using a ladle, fill each of the jars to within ¼ inch of the top of the jar. Yes, it's important to be exact. With a hot damp rag, wipe the rims and threads of each jar to clean them. They must be clean of spilled jelly. Take your lids and place them on each jar, then screw the rings down over them hand tight, and then set them back on the towel.

Remember the kettle that you sterilized your jars in? Crank the heat back up under it and bring it back to a boil. While it's heating, slip your jars into the rack, one at a time with the jar lifters. Once it boils, let it boil for 5 minutes, then turn off the heat and remove the jars one at a time, putting them upright on the towel again.

And now you wait. What you just did is called "water bath canning". The heated jelly pulls a vacuum on the lids as it cools, excluding air and bacteria and whatnot. Over the next few hours, you will hear "plink!" again and again as the lids seal. You can tell the lid has sealed when you can push on the middle of the lid and it does not move. If it allows you to push and it pops back out, it hasn't sealed yet. Let them cool for six hours (or overnight) before you put them in the pantry, after you make sure all the lids are sealed. If any didn't seal by the next morning, just put those in the fridge and use them first.

The sealed ones will last at room temperature in your pantry for years. If you had one jar that didn't quite get filled, don't bother canning it; just put it in the fridge as is.

This basic formula - five cups of juice, six cups of sugar, and one package of Sure Jell, will make jelly from just about anything. Hot peppers, plums, peaches, strawberries ... almost anything. Water bath canning works perfectly for this kind of jelly, too. You process it for five minutes for a half-pint jar, and 10 minutes for a pint jar—at least, that is, if you are less than 1,000 feet above sea level. Check the pectin package if you are higher than that for the right processing times.

It's a lot to write it out, but it's not much work - not really. Most of it is waiting. But when you spread some muscadine jelly on a biscuit or a piece of toast this winter, when you have cabin fever and the warmth of August feels so far away, you will remember that thicket, and you will not begrudge the time at all.

Muscadine jelly

Ingredients

- 5 cups fresh muscadine juice (about 5 pounds of muscadines)

- 6 cups of sugar

- 11.75 ounce package of pectin

Wash the muscadines, put them in a large pot and add water to cover. Bring the pot to a full boil. Reduce heat to a simmer and cook for 30-40 minutes, occasionally mashing the muscadines with a potato masher.

Take the pot off the stove and then pour mashed muscadines and juice into your chinois, which you have placed in a large bowl. Allow it a few minutes to drain, then work the chinois to mash all the pulp, extracting every bit of juice you can.

Line a colander with cheesecloth, and then pour the juice and pulp into it, allowing it to drain for several hours. Do NOT mash or squeeze the pulp.

Put the juice in a large stockpot and bring it to a rolling boil you can't stir down. Then reduce to a simmer. When simmering, add the pectin and stir until it's dissolved, then bring the juice back to a rolling boil and boil it for one minute. Then add the sugar, stirring it in until it's dissolved. Bring the juice back to a rolling boil and boil it for one minute, stirring constantly. Then remove it from the heat.

Using a slotted spoon, skim the foam from the top of the juice, then using a ladle, pour the jelly into hot sterilized jars, filling the jar, but leaving a ¼ inch of space. Screw the two-piece lids onto the jars.

Place the jars into a water bath canner with enough simmering water to cover the jars by 2 inches. Bring it to a boil and keep it there for five minutes*. Remove the jars from the water using jar lifters (be careful—this is all hot!) and put them on a dish towel to cool. Do not move the jars for 6-8 hours or, ideally, overnight. Before storing, make sure the jar is sealed by checking the lids—sealed jars will have the center of the lid fully depressed; on unsealed ones you can depress the center of the lid. Store unsealed jars in the refrigerator; sealed ones go in the pantry.

* *The directions are for sea level or thereabouts—if you are over 1,000 ft above sea level, consult the pectin package for processing times.*

29

A MOVEABLE FEAST

It is common for people who write memoirs about their impoverished childhood to said things like, "We were poor, but didn't know we were."

I knew how poor we were. I was aware of how poor the people around us were. I knew that parking on a hill and pushing the truck and popping the clutch to get the truck started because we couldn't afford to get the starter replaced was not how people in the books I read, people I saw on movies on TV, people who lived in cities lived. But that was how we lived.

And so, like poor people have since time immemorial, we often made gifts to give the people we cared about, instead of buying them at stores.

My Aunt Louise had lived through the Depression, and she carefully saved the gift wrap from every present to be reused next year. She had a hatbox full of bows and ribbon she had saved from previous years' gifts. More than once, my birthday present was wrapped in the Sunday comics, and even at 7 I knew she had chosen the Sunday comics because they were more colorful, and she had gone to the extra pains because I was loved.

Aunt Monty saved Christmas and birthday cards and would remove the front and reuse it as its own card—sort of a Christmas postcard. My momma to this very day has a stash of gift bags for all occasions from earlier celebrations.

I don't recall thinking any of this was weird. But normal is always another word for whatever you are used to.

Because things were so tight, there were some folks you got store-bought gifts for, but most everyone else got made gifts, often food. And because my daddy was a popular man, we got all sorts of food gifts during the holidays.

There was the Chex Mix, the puppy chow (which was a sort of chocolate covered Chex Mix), the caramel popcorn and the peanut brittle. But my favorite was the Christmas fudge.

The Christmas fudge always showed up the week after Thanksgiving. It was a slower time back then, and holidays stayed in their own spaces—these days, you see Santa Claus in ads before Halloween is over.

But that Sunday after Thanksgiving, you were subject to being gifted a tin of Christmas fudge if you lingered too long after church. Folk had made a batch the day before and were aching to give it out.

Sometimes it was wrapped in a small box like a present, other times wrapped in wax paper with a sticker to hold it shut, but my favorite was always when it was in a small tin box.

I have in adulthood bought Christmas tins at the dollar store, but I never remember them being on the shelves then. They just showed up, and once they were gifted to us with fudge in them, we would save them, to be sent out next year, filled with fudge for someone else. Sometimes, you would release a Christmas tin into the community, only to get the same one back two to three years later from a different family, with paint chips along the edges, a bit scruffier, but still welcomed like an old friend bearing gifts.

I have always struggled to grow fingernails of any length, so seven-year-old me would struggle to open the fudge tin—the outside was slick and the lip on the lid small, so I always felt a bit like I was wrestling it to gain access to its treasures. About one out of three times I would end up dropping it, to make a resounding clatter that echoed throughout the house and put shot my idea of surreptitious fudge eating.

But the act of opening that tin, once you got it open, was magical. The smell hit you first, then the sight of the opaque, creased wax paper that the tin had been lined with, which you then unfolded to reveal the small blocks of fudge.

Some folks sought extra credit by putting nuts in their fudge. These people were my heroes, elevating an already excellent treat to the extraordinary. Most recipes these days call for walnuts, and we saw some of that. But many of us had pecan trees in our yards, and after all, fudge was the gift poor folks gave each other, so the free pecans often won out over the purchased walnuts. One lady at church always used whole walnut halves, one placed on top of each square of fudge, as if she were John D. Rockefeller's wife and had not a care in the world. But they had a black walnut tree on their property, and so all the walnuts had cost them was the clothes-staining work of husking and then shelling them by busting them with a hammer. Wealth takes many forms, and not all of them have to do with money.

As a boy who would find myself free from school obligations over Christmas break, I would make rounds in the neighborhood, strategically trying to get offered Christmas treats of all sorts, but especially fudge. Almost every house had some, and if you were visiting, some would almost always be offered. It was like a moveable feast, a traveling dessert tray, a sugar-laden smorgasbord, where the pure variety of all the goodness was offered.

Christmas was a magical time to be a boy.

These days, we don't get many gifts of food—I'm not sure why that is. I suspect it means the capitalists have won by convincing us that store-bought gifts are superior to homemade gifts, but it's hard to put as much love into a hair dryer or a porcelain knickknack as it is a tin of fudge. It also means you don't have a stash of Christmas tins in your hall closet. So, most years around Thanksgiving, I haunt the dollar stores, looking for colorful tins to pack with fudge to give to people I love.

In my collection of recipes from those days, I cannot find a canonical, agreed-upon way to make fudge, and mom made it different ways different times, but the recipients were always happy to get it, no matter how it was made.

This is how I make it, but I'm sure yours is good, too, and the people who receive it will be just as delighted with fudge made from the recipe on the back of the marshmallow bag as they will some artisanal fudge made by a recipe from the old country. As always, love is the key ingredient.

Anytime you make candy, it scares some folks. But it's not hard, just involved, the same way that a pot of pinto beans is not involved. You can't drift off while making it. But the reward for that much attention is pretty high.

To make fudge, all we're going to do is melt sugar, butter, evaporated milk and a bit of salt until it gets to 234 degrees. While it's melting, you must stir it to keep it all incorporated. I said 234 degrees, mind: not 230, and not 240. 234, exactly.

Then you are going to pull it off the heat and immediately (immediately, I said!) add marshmallows and chocolate and then whisk it like your life depends on it for at least a minute, maybe two, until the chocolate is all melted and the marshmallows are incorporated. This is why it's important to chop up the chocolate before you get started—it melts more easily. Finally, add your nuts if you are a nut person.

Once that's done, you pour the mix into a sling-lined pan. Now, sometimes you see a thing on the internet, and it amazes you that you never thought of it before—for me, that is an aluminum foil sling. Basically, you tear off a sheet of foil about half again as long as your baking dish, then you fold it to the width of the dish and lay it over it. Then do that again but lay this second one on top of, but perpendicular to, the first. Then mash them both into the pan, fitting it down into the corners. Now, when all is done, you just lift on the bottom piece of foil and you have handles to remove the entire block of fudge up in one motion. If I lost you, just go on YouTube and search for "aluminum foil sling". There's lots of people out there now preaching this gospel.

After you get your fudge mix into the baking dish, tuck it into the refrigerator for a couple of hours to set up, then remove and allow it to sit 10-15 minutes before slicing it—it slices better and neater that way. If your fudge is too cold, it will crumble when you slice it. It will still taste good, but it won't be as pretty.

If you are giving this as a gift, I always line the tin or box with wax paper first, then the fudge, stacked nice and neat, and then more wax paper.

Christmas fudge

Ingredients

- 3 cups light brown sugar

- 12 tablespoons of butter, cut into pieces

- ⅔ cup evaporated milk

- ½ teaspoon salt

- 12 ounces chopped 60% bittersweet chocolate bar

- 5 ounces large marshmallows (around 20-22 of the regular size)

- 1 ½ cups chopped walnuts (optional)

Special equipment:

A candy thermometer (regular or digital—both are cheap these days, and worth having)

Make a foil sling for your 8x8 baking pan, laying two layers of aluminum foil crossways and pressing into the corners. Then, grease the foil with butter or vegetable spray.

In a large saucepan, combine the first four ingredients, bringing them to a boil while stirring frequently. When boiling, reduce heat to low and simmer (while still stirring often) until the mixture reaches 234 degrees. Immediately remove from the heat.

Now add the chocolate and marshmallows, stirring it in until well mixed – this is going to take a few minutes. Some folks will want to use beaters here. When done, it will have the consistency of frosting. Stir in nuts if using, then put the mixture into your baking pan, and let cool for at least two hours in the refrigerator. Remove from the refrigerator and allow to sit at room temp for 10 minutes, then cut into 1-inch cubes. It can be kept at room temperature for a few weeks, but it never lasts that long in our house.

30

SAME AS IT EVER WAS

As I write this on the last day of October of 2025, the government in the US is shut down, and the Republican administration is refusing to authorize emergency spending to keep SNAP benefits (we used to call these food stamps) active next month.

In other words, beginning tomorrow, some 40 million Americans are going to not have enough money to feed their families. Rather than be horrified that 40 million people need help to feed themselves and their families in a country as prosperous as the US, politicians are using these people as pawns in their attempts to get their own pet projects passed. Meanwhile, children and elderly folks and just folks are going to go hungry.

The people who support not giving aid to folks who need it are always cloaked in morality. Stories come out about people who use SNAP benefits to buy beef, or candy, or, heaven forfend, a box of cake mix. Somebody who hasn't eaten a lentil in a decade will chime in about how much cheaper it is to buy lentils than meat, and if only these poor people knew what they knew, they wouldn't be poor.

Meanwhile, we are in a period of inflation, and groceries are outrageously expensive. Even those of us who do not rely on SNAP are having to cut back on the food we buy at the grocery store.

Now, it's dangerous to put dates and events in a book such as this, lest it seem out of date. But the thing is, somebody, somewhere, is always politicizing and weaponizing food.

I come from working-class folks. We got USDA commodities when I was a kid in the 80s–I still have dreams about how good the grilled cheese sandwiches were that were made from government cheese.

We had a garden, where my momma tended her tomato and pepper plants, and every winter we ate off the jarred and frozen produce we had put by. We would go to the store on Mondays to buy the leftover Sunday papers to get extras of the coupons in the circulars. She knew what day the butcher reduced prices on the unsold meat, and I ate my body weight each month in chicken leg quarters, which were always on sale. Oatmeal in the meatloaf made it go further.

We never went hungry, but it was close sometimes, and more than once we were saved because a neighbor shared their excess with us—not charity, mind you—they just had extra, and wondered if we could use it?

The food I have written about in these pages is, for the most part the food eaten by poor hill country folks in the Southern US. This was not the food of luxury but was often the food of celebration. We celebrated with chocolate cake and fried chicken and chicken and dressing. It wasn't the cost of the food that made it celebratory; it was the love that went into it that did.

I am now, in my sixth decade, aware of how limited the palate was. We relied more on fat and less on spices for flavor. Other than cayenne pepper, black pepper, salt, vanilla, and cinnamon, our spice rack was relatively empty. We mostly fried, braised, or boiled things—cooking methods that either went really fast, or that went really slow and unattended, so you could do other things. There is a reason we never ate risotto—nobody had time to do all that stirring.

As I look back through the recipes I included, I notice that while they are accurate; they are not how we really cook. They are more prescriptive, authoritative, top-down. Meanwhile, we see them mostly as jumping-off points.

If it's deep into winter and you need a dessert to take to the church potluck, maybe you don't have blackberries for a cobbler, but you have a few cans of peaches in the back of the pantry. Peach cobbler it is!

Or it's a tight month and you are out of chicken, so you use the breakfast sausage you had in the freezer in the dressing instead. Depending on the vagaries of the pantry, the budget, and your own taste, the beef soup becomes chicken soup, the cheese omelet becomes a mushroom omelet, the creamed chicken over toast becomes creamed beef over rice. If you know how to make pinto beans or black-eyed peas, you know how to make baby Limas, too.

Recipes are just a structure, a framework, on which you can hang the ingredients you have available. In fact, in writing the book, I don't really have the expectation that you will cook the food I talk about here. In a real sense, it's a metaphor, a conceit, a literary device to get you to think about the food that matters to you, and that makes you feel loved and safe and cared for.

I don't know what those foods are for you, but these are mine, and if you are lacking in food that equals love to you, I offer you these as a starting point.

The main thing, though, whether you make these meals or the ones from your own family's canon, is to keep the chain going. Long after the taste fades, the memories remain.

About the Author

Hugh Hollowell is a southern writer who lives in Jackson, Mississippi. A sixth-generation Mississippian, he currently serves as the senior pastor of Open Door Mennonite Church in Jackson, Mississippi—a peace and justice church formed in the aftermath of the Civil Rights movement.

As an active storyteller and speaker, his writing has been featured in national publications such as *The Washington Post*, *Sojourners*, and *The Huffington Post*, and he has lectured at various universities including Duke, Occidental College, and Swarthmore College.

Besides his pastoral and advocacy work, he publishes a long-running weekly newsletter titled *Life Is So Beautiful*, where he shares hopeful essays and curated links. Hollowell lives in the Fondren neighborhood of Jackson, Mississippi, with his wife, Renee. Together, they co-parent five cats and four chickens.

To find out what he's up to, to order signed books, or to stalk him on social media, find him at hughhollowell.org.

www.ingramcontent.com/pod-product-compliance
Lightning Source LLC
Chambersburg PA
CBHW060419130626
46555CB00005B/2129

* 9 7 9 8 9 9 9 4 0 5 8 7 0 1 *